FROM SURVIVING TO THRIVING

"The journey of Rebuilding Relationships After Trauma"

Hubert Sugira Hategekimana

All Rights Reserved © 2024 by Hubert Sugira Hategekimana.

Cover Design by: Noella Habarugira

No part of this book may be reproduced or transmitted in any form or by any means, graphic, electronic, or mechanical, including photocopying, recording, taping, internet, or by any information storage retrieval system, without written permission of the publisher, King's Way Media.

Scripture quoted by permission. Quotations designated (NET) are from the NET Bible® copyright ©1996-2016 by Biblical Studies Press, L.L.C. http://netbible.org All rights reserved.

King's Way Media
40C Henderson Ave
Ottawa - ON K1N 7P1
CANADA

ISBN: 978-0-9959245-1-2

Printed in East Africa

This Edition Printing: September 2024

The book cover features a serene sky-blue backdrop adorned with graceful birds soaring freely, symbolizing liberation and the boundless potential for growth and transformation. Amidst this tranquil scene, a few white clouds drift gently, symbolizing the challenges and obstacles one encounters on the journey of healing and self-discovery. However, the presence of these clouds alongside the expansive blue sky also suggests that these challenges are temporary and can be overcome.

At the heart of the cover, a face gazes resolutely forward, subtly merging with the intricate branches of a flourishing tree. This visual metaphor encapsulates the profound resilience and inner strength that defines the human spirit. This cover conjures up the image of a tiny seed germination beneath the soil, eventually sprouting into a majestic tree, resilient and steadfast despite adversity, as inspiration for the empowering quote, "They tried to bury us, but they didn't know we were seeds."

This symbolism speaks to the theme of thriving in the face of challenges, embodying the notion that the capacity for profound inner growth and renewal exists even amidst darkness.

The juxtaposition of the face's outward expression with the tree's internal growth highlights the journey of self-discovery and empowerment beneath the surface.

As the birds take flight against the backdrop of an expansive sky, they symbolize the ultimate expression of freedom and possibility, inviting you to embark on a transformative journey of healing, self-discovery, and empowerment.

After reading this book...

"Hubert Sugira is a hero for speaking the unspeakable, giving it the right words, and opening up lives. His courage in writing about what many cannot address shows the deep value he places on helping others in their journey of healing.

Hubert embodies peace, which is evident in the way he inspires others to seek it as well. True leadership, as he demonstrates, is about guiding others toward goodness without keeping it to oneself. His work reminds us that the world is full of goodness, but it requires selfless individuals like Hubert to share it with others to prevent conflict.

The unspeakable pain of the 1994 Genocide against the Tutsi became a path that revealed extraordinary gifts within those who endured it, turning them into channels of blessing for many. Hubert's ability to transform his own story into a source of strength for others is a testament to his character and his calling.

Hubert is a blessing not only to Rwanda but to the entire world because he looks beyond himself to care for others. His work reflects the belief that true happiness is found in the desire to see others happy. It's not the many years that make one impactful, but the love and dedication put into the work. I encourage Hubert to continue sharing his wisdom and pray for him as he leads others on this path. I also urge him to translate this book into Kinyarwanda to help his people, who need healing and strength to rise from their wounds.

This book is a valuable tool for researchers and will help me personally in accompanying families and those in need of healing and resilience.

Long live, Hubert, and may your work continue to light the way for many."

Sr. Immaculée Uwamariya
Bernardine Sisters
Founder of Famille Espérance
Headmistress of Collège St Bernard Kansi
Member of the Youth and Family Commission in the Catholic Church of Rwanda

DEDICATION

I dedicate this book to all the victims of the 1994 Genocide against Tutsi in my beloved country of Rwanda, especially my family members, like:

My grandma, Cansilda Mukantagara, who, after she was wounded, I had to leave behind when I was running for my own life. She had just been macheted and was unconscious, lying down in her own blood. A group of neighbors had attacked my grandma, who was in her 70s or 80s and had a house in our compound. She had lost her sight and was not leaving the house because of her condition.

What I remember about her is that she loved me so dearly that I was the kid for whom she had a special salutation: "Uri igisheja, gishengera gishaka, kitashaka kigashora inka rugarama." What she may have meant is that she saw in me that I was to become a man of principle who would only entertain what he wanted. Grandma had seen me through.

I remember that my parents could not punish me. I used to run into her house and jump into her bed, and nobody dared come for me there.

Grandma, your igisheja now has a son of the same age as when you last saw him. You would be very proud of me.

Just before the attack on our family on April 8, 1994, the last conversation my mum had with my grandma was that she wanted us to run to the Belgians UN Peacekeepers who were stationed at ETO (Technical School) Kicukiro, not far from our house.

In the past, like in 1959 or the 60ies when Tutsi were hunted down, those who found refuge at ETO were saved. My grandma was pleading to be taken there, but my mum refused because she was 8 months pregnant. My mum had resolved to die in her own house. The last words my grandma told my mum was that "*Inyamaswa ntindi, ibyara umuhigo wahagurutse,*" meaning that an animal that will not see its better days will give birth when it is hunting time. Those are the last words my mum heard just a few minutes before the Interwahamwe came and macheted her.

Karasira Remy, my cousin, and best friend, was one year older than me. One day, they separated us in kindergarten, so each one went with his agemates. I left the class as if I were going to the washroom and walked 30 minutes back home all by myself at four years old, just because I did not want to stay in a class if he was not in it.

Karasira Clement was very quiet and an outstanding football player with fantastic dribbling. After the UN Belgian soldiers at the school I told you my grandma wanted to join left them behind, they did not survive the mass killing of the Tutsi in Nyanza-Kicukiro on April 11, 1994.

I also dedicate this book to their mom, my aunt, Astherie Bazizane. She was a sweet soul, loved people, and always had a smile on her face. She used to give me live chickens to keep, but because we were close neighbors, they would always return to her house.

My uncle Rwabarindwa Frédéric's family (Aunt Asterie, cousins, Umuhire delta, Kimenyi Olivier, Umurungi Oliva, Sano Gaston, Byusa Dominique Savio, nobody knows where they are buried as for now

My uncle Gapita's family (Aunt Uzamukunda Dorothee, cousins Gapita Theophile, Gapita Jacqueline, Gapita Theoneste, Gapita Christine, Gapita Octave, Gapita Obert, and Uwineza Clemence) was wiped out. As time passes, I have a hard time remembering your faces. We did not keep any pictures except one of Theophile, who was an acrobat at Gatenga, and they once went to represent the country in Italy; oh, how the whole village was proud.

Our friends who had become like family, Murego Faustin, Uwamariya Felicite, Murego Fernard & Murego Herve

Our next-door neighbors who had become like family: Bwanakweli Charles, Munyawera Policarpe, Kayitesi Clotilde, Uwera Marie Claudette, Mutesi Marie Claudine, na Munyawera Gatete Mon-fort, and so many others I will not be able to list in this book. You are always in our memories, and we tell our kids about you and the good times we had together.

One of my classmates, neighbors, and friends, Kevin Kabenga, I remember that I used to come and wait for you so we could go to school together after stopping by your parent's shop and grabbing a bottle of Fanta Orange for the road.

I also dedicate this book to all of you who survived the 94 genocide against the Tutsi; your resilience and dedication to doing your best to thrive and rebuild your life in this almost impossible life is an example that nothing is impossible.

I also want to dedicate this book to all of you who have given yourself tirelessly to stop the genocide, Inkotanyi, young men and women who have risked all to save others and give us a country where every Rwandan can thrive and make it, mwarakoze nkotanyi, gutanga ubuzima (thanks for giving us back life)

TABLE OF CONTENTS

ACKNOWLEDGEMENTS	11
FOREWORD	13
PREFACE	17
INTRODUCTION	25
CHAPTER 1 - IMPACT OF TRAUMA ON YOUR RELATIONSHIPS	31
CHAPTER 2 - REBUILDING YOUR IDENTITY & SELF-IMAGE	46
CHAPTER 3 - HEALING FAMILY BONDS	105
CHAPTER 4 - NAVIGATING SPOUSAL RELATIONSHIPS	123
CHAPTER 5 - CULTIVATING TRUST IN FRIENDSHIPS	165
CHAPTER 6 - BALANCING PERSONAL & PROFESSIONAL LIFE	179
CHAPTER 7 - BUILDING POSITIVE ACQUANTANCESHIPS	189
CHAPTER 8 - THE HEALING JOURNEY: STRATEGIES & PRACTICES	197
CHAPTER 9 - CONCLUSION	225
HUBERT'S BIOGRAPHY	229

ACKNOWLEDGEMENTS

This book would not be possible without Rwanda's excellent national leadership, which brought back to life a country that was a total failure 30 years ago. Thank you, Perezida wacu, your Excellence Paul Kagame, and your whole team for deciding to build a united nation where our kids will grow without having to respond in classes if they are Tutsi, Hutu, or Twa. Still, we are, above all, Rwandans.

Thank you to all of you, especially the survivors, who have shown us that even in the face of unimaginable adversity, hope can be rekindled, and great things can be achieved. I am also grateful to my fellow authors and speakers like Dimitri, Claver, Akariza, Ancilla, and Ngabo Brave, who have challenged me to see life in a whole different way in the last few days—mukomeze mudadire.

Thanks to the Zillionizer and the Kigali Family Night team for your unwavering support. Your belief in me and dedication to bringing out all that God has entrusted to me is commendable. You guys are the backbone of this project.

Thanks to Noella for imagining and crafting this excellent book cover.

Thanks to Vital for sleepless nights collecting and putting together all the content.

My purpose partner Emmanuel, we will definitely see the vision come to pass.

Thank you to the Karangwa family, Olivier, and Carine, for being who you are—a fantastic support system.

Thanks to my bonus American parents, the Pitts, Leslie, and Graham, for making me feel loved for who I am. Thank you for providing a perfect, quiet space for me while putting the ideas of this book on pages and taking care of me during the whole process. May your work, support, and dedication be remembered in generations to come

Thanks to my spiritual covering and parents, Pastor Lynell and Dr. Martin Williams, for showing me the way and keeping me in check.

My family is always there to guide and support me, no matter what is at stake; having you in my life is a blessing.

My wife Jennifer, who has seen the worst and best version of myself and yet stuck around and has given me the best kids in the world, Kayla, Ketsia, and Klemes, I pray that you will grow in a different nation as we did grow into and believe that you will give a better legacy to your children.

Last but not least, I beg forgiveness from all of you who have been with me over the course of the years and whose names I have failed to mention. You are dear to me.

FOREWORD

It was 11:30 at night on November 7, 2011. My husband, Graham, and I were in the Bahamas as long-time trustees for Dr. Myles Munroe's International Leadership organization. Due to rich back-to-back meetings throughout the day, we'd not stopped to eat since lunchtime. The evening session adjourning, we headed to a take-out window at the restaurant of the hosting hotel only to discover that the food service hours had just ended with the gentleman customer in front of us receiving the last order of the day before closing.

It was a moment of destiny. That customer was the 28-year-old Hubert Sugira Hategekimana. He had overheard our being turned away and, surprisingly and generously, offered us his dinner that he was carrying away in a to-go bag. Who would do such a thing? Who was this young man?

We politely declined his offer, after which my husband struck up a conversation to ask our fellow conference attendee a bit about his story. Hubert initially responded that he lived in Ottawa. My husband probed. He further revealed that his original home was in Rwanda. When we asked if he had been living there during the '94 genocide, we were moved to hear that at age 11, he had lived through the 100 days of horrific atrocities, having lost many beloved family members and friends. Now living in Canada, Hubert has become a participant in Dr. Myles Munroe's online mentoring program, intently studying and digesting Dr. Munroe's messages about purpose, identity, and leadership.

The following day, it was our privilege and joy to personally introduce Hubert to his mentor, whose words and ideas had been vitally transformative to his understanding of his own identity and his search for meaning and purpose in his journey.

From that point forward, Hubert used his gifts to serve Dr. Munroe, becoming a trusted companion into whom his mentor poured the essence of his life's discoveries and understanding. Ultimately, Dr. Munroe commissioned, authorized, and released Hubert to himself, taking up the baton to teach these transformational truths, now embodied in Hubert's own life and delivered through his voice and his experience.

Today, he continues offering a meal to you, the reader. "From Surviving to Thriving: The Journey of Rebuilding Relationships After Trauma" is Hubert's gift to you. He has refined his talents, tested his principles, curated transformational truths, and offers himself to you in your journey of self-discovery, purpose, and meaning.

Having intently devoted hundreds of hours to listening to stories of the pain of fellow survivors of the genocide, he offers healing principles that relate to the individual, to the collective pain of a greater community, and, ultimately, to the world.

In the pages ahead, you will delve into:
how to discover your true identity,
how to work through individual and generational trauma,
how to disempower the impact of trauma on your relationships,
how to nourish your most crucial community - the family,
how to repair and forge a stronger, more healthy marriage.

Having been trained in the healing profession as a trauma counselor and licensed marriage and family therapist, I am always in awe of humans' healing capacity.

Trauma is an agonizing assault on the deepest parts of our being, whether physical or emotional. Our safety is shattered, our sense of self reduced to helplessness, and our entire nervous system reverberates with fight, flight, or freeze. Triggers can jolt us back within a split second to a felt bodily sense of violation.

FOREWORD

I have found through my practice of serving those working through trauma that most of us manage our pain in one of three main ways.

One tendency can be to push our pain down inside ourselves, where we have to numb ourselves to keep pain out of our immediate consciousness. The behaviors we use to accomplish that—distraction, drinking, busyness, substance abuse, spending, avoidance, addictions, and detachment— serve to alleviate the pain for a while but ultimately may result in sickness in our bodies.

A second tendency can be to push our pain away from ourselves in blame. Focusing our pain on the fault and guilt of others leaves us with a sense of disempowerment as victims, harboring what can become destructive bitterness. This may leave us sick in our souls.

So what can we do with our pain if we don't push it down or push it away?

Hubert's book gives us a pathway to avoid being stuck. He shows us that a healing journey comes through processing our pain, gaining courage to find our voices and speak our losses, connecting with our emotions of grief, mourning and searching for meaning and purpose, discovering how we have learned and grown, and finding new hope.

Hubert invites us to accompany him on a path of self-discovery, an invitation to new perspective, and ultimately, breaking past simply surviving our pain to actually thriving in our relationships—with ourselves first and then in our relationships with others.

Having read this manuscript, I would not add one thing to its content as a manual and map for healing in our relationships. Hubert is a trusted guide and an accomplished teacher. Savor the meal he is sharing with you and be challenged, strengthened, and transformed by his words.

Leslie Laughlin Pitt, MA
Licensed Marriage and Therapist
North Carolina, USA

Hubert, the day he met his mentor, the Late Dr. Myles Munroe, for the first time

PREFACE

While this book may have been written to help survivors of the 1994 genocide against the Tutsi in Rwanda, its themes and insights are likely to resonate with anyone who has experienced a wide range of traumatic events and is seeking to heal and rebuild their life and relationships with a sense of purpose and significance.

Genocide is the deliberate and systematic extermination of a particular national, racial, ethnic, or religious group. Raphael Lemkin coined the term in 1944, combining the Greek word "genos" (meaning "race" or "tribe") with the Latin word "cide" (meaning "killing"). Genocide encompasses a range of acts like direct killing, mass execution, torture, rape, and so many atrocities committed with the intent to destroy, in whole or in part, a specific group of people.

Numerous international treaties and conventions, such as the Convention on the Prevention and Punishment of the Crime of Genocide that the United Nations General Assembly adopted in 1948, prohibit the most severe crime under international law: genocide. International tribunals, domestic courts, or procedures like truth commissions and reconciliation processes can all prosecute and hold genocide perpetrators accountable.

Now, the 94 Genocide against the Tutsi in Rwanda is even more complex and worse because of its:

1. Scale, Speed, and Animosity The genocide against the Tutsi in 1994 unfolded with astonishing speed, resulting in the mass slaughter of more than 1,000,000 Tutsi within just three months; that is, around 10,000 people were killed every day for 100 days. If we look at the 94 genocide against the Tutsi in numbers, it wiped out 75% of the Tutsi population, where around 300,000 children were killed, around 100,000 children were orphaned, one-third of whom witnessed the death of their families, and 96% witnessed violence. 31% of child survivors witnessed a rape. An estimated 100,000-250,000 women were raped during the three months of the genocide, with 70% of which were infected by HIV & AIDS; 20,000 children were born to these women as a result of rape. All of these crimes were intended to terrorize the Tutsi population, break up families, destroy communities, and have definitely changed the makeup of the next generations. For example, many raped women are now incapable of bearing more children. The sheer scale and intensity of the violence shocked the world and highlighted the catastrophic consequences of unchecked ethnic hatred.
2. Proximity or Role of Ordinary Citizens: Unlike many other genocides, the 94 genocide against the Tutsi was characterized by the widespread participation of ordinary civilians in the perpetration of killing and violence. Neighbors turned against neighbors, colleagues against colleagues, and even family members participated in the slaughter, illustrating the depth of societal breakdown and moral collapse.
3. Ethnic Dimension(or lack of it): The 94 genocide was primarily driven by the ethnic hatred of the extremist Hutu with a systematic targeting of Tutsi civilians, as well as

INTRODUCTION

moderate Hutu who opposed the extremist ideology or who helped Tutsi were killed, but the target was clearly the Tutsi, that is why we can not call it how we want, or Rwandan genocide because the target was not a group called Rwandans, the 94 genocide against Tutsi reflected long-standing tensions and animosities exacerbated by colonial legacies and political manipulation.

The uniqueness of the Rwandan setup is that you can not really talk about ethnic groups because, by definition, An ethnic group is a social category of people who share a common cultural heritage, ancestry, language, religion, or other cultural traits. Members of an ethnic group typically identify with each other based on a sense of belonging and shared identity that distinguishes them from different groups within a society.

While Hutu and Tutsi have historically been considered separate ethnic groups in Rwanda and Burundi, this classification is not entirely accurate. It can oversimplify the social and cultural dynamics of these societies. Here are some reasons why it can be problematic to categorize Hutu and Tutsi strictly as ethnic groups:

Shared Ancestry and Intermarriage: Historically, Hutu and Tutsi have shared common ancestry and cultural practices. Intermarriage between Hutu and Tutsi has been common, blurring the lines between the two groups and challenging rigid ethnic distinctions.

Hutu and Tutsi identities have been fluid and socially constructed in Rwandan and Burundian societies, influenced by socioeconomic status, political affiliation, and historical circumstances. Individuals and families could move between Hutu and Tutsi categories based on changes in social status or political alliances.

Colonial Influence: Belgium's imposition of colonial rule in Rwanda and Burundi exacerbated ethnic tensions and reinforced distinctions between Hutu and Tutsi. Belgian colonial administrators implemented policies that categorized people based on physical characteristics and socioeconomic status, further entrenching ethnic divisions.

Political Manipulation: Ethnic identities in Rwanda and Burundi have been manipulated for political purposes, particularly during periods of colonial rule and post-independence governance. Political leaders have exploited Hutu-Tutsi divisions to consolidate power, incite violence, and perpetuate discrimination.

Holistic Cultural Identity: Hutu and Tutsi identities encompass more than just ethnic categorization; they also include linguistic, cultural, and historical dimensions. In Rwanda, there was no Hutu or distinct Tutsi language or culture. Given these complexities, scholars and analysts like:

Mahmood Mamdani, a Ugandan academic and political commentator, has written extensively on the politics of identity and violence in Africa. In his book "When Victims Become Killers: Colonialism, Nativism, and the Genocide in Rwanda," Mamdani explores how colonialism and the imposition of ethnic categories by European colonizers contributed to the construction of Hutu and Tutsi identities as political rather than purely ethnic categories.

Scott Straus, an American political scientist specializing in African politics, has also examined the fluidity and political manipulation of Hutu and Tutsi identities in Rwanda. His work, including the book "The Order of Genocide: Race, Power, and War in Rwanda," analyzes how political elites and colonial powers have instrumentalized ethnic identities for their interests, leading to cycles of violence and conflict.

Catharine Newbury, an American historian and expert on African politics, has written extensively on ethnicity and conflict in Rwanda and Burundi. In her book "The Cohesion of Oppression: Clientship and Ethnicity in Rwanda, 1860–1960," Newbury explores the historical evolution of Hutu and Tutsi identities and argues that these identities were shaped by political and socioeconomic factors rather than fixed ethnic categories.

These scholars' works offer valuable insights into the complex and nuanced nature of Hutu and Tutsi identities, highlighting the importance of historical context, political dynamics, and social processes in understanding these categories.

According to Mr. Aimable Havugiyaremye, the Prosecutor General of Rwanda (in his speech at Kwibuka30, Nyanza-Kicukiro, on April 11, 2024), the denial of the 94 Genocide against the Tutsi in Rwanda reached a point where, in the ICTR, the defense argued that Tutsi were not a protected ethnic group.

It is easier to view Hutu and Tutsi identities as social constructs shaped by historical, political, and socioeconomic factors rather than fixed ethnic categories. Recognizing the fluidity and complexity of Hutu and Tutsi identities can help foster a more nuanced understanding of the dynamics at play in Rwandan and Burundian societies and promote reconciliation and peace-building efforts.

The 1994 genocide against the Tutsi was fueled by hate propaganda disseminated through radio broadcasts and other media outlets. Radio stations like Radio Télévision Libre des Mille Collines (RTLM) played a central role in dehumanizing Tutsi and encouraging violence against them, contributing to the rapid spread of genocidal ideology.

4. *International Response and Failure:* The 94 genocide against the Tutsi in Rwanda exposed the catastrophic failure of the international community to intervene and prevent mass atrocities. Despite early warnings and evidence of genocide, the United Nations and individual countries failed to respond effectively, leading to widespread condemnation and soul-searching about the responsibility to protect.

The genocide against the Tutsi in Rwanda remains one of the darkest chapters in recent history, highlighting the catastrophic consequences of ethnic hatred, political manipulation, and international inaction. It serves as a stark reminder of the importance of promoting peace, reconciliation, and justice to prevent such atrocities from occurring in the future.

As a relationship expert who has dedicated my career to helping individuals navigate the complexities of family, marriage, and various interpersonal connections, I've become acutely aware of the pervasive yet often unaddressed issues that linger in our society. Among these, one stands out prominently: the profound and lasting impact of the 94 genocide against the Tutsi on today's relationships.

Over the years, as I've worked closely with individuals and families, I've observed a common thread weaving through many of their challenges—a thread intricately linked to the collective trauma of our past. This thread manifests in strained marriages, fractured families, and individuals struggling to find their footing in the world. And yet, it's a thread that often goes unnoticed or unacknowledged in our day-to-day conversations about relationships and well-being.

Introduction

In writing this book, I aim to illuminate this overlooked aspect of our collective experience and explore its profound implications for our lives and relationships. It's a journey that invites us to confront uncomfortable truths, unpack the complexities of trauma and resilience, and chart a course toward healing and transformation.

Through the pages that follow, we will delve into the depths of trauma—the scars it leaves, the challenges it poses, and the resilience it engenders. We will examine how the legacy of the 94 genocide against the Tutsi trauma continues to shape our identities, our relationships, and our communities, often in ways we may not fully grasp.

But this book is not merely about dwelling on the wounds of the past; it's about illuminating a path forward—a path toward healing, understanding, and growth. It's about reclaiming agency, rewriting the narratives that bind us, and forging new connections based on empathy, compassion, and shared humanity.

Drawing from my own experience and those close to me, my professional expertise, and the wisdom gleaned from countless individuals who have bravely shared their stories, we will explore practical strategies for rebuilding relationships, fostering resilience, and nurturing thriving communities.

We will confront the challenges head-on and celebrate the triumphs, resilience, and unwavering spirit that persist in the face of adversity.

Additionally, we will delve into the phenomenon of transgenerational transmission of trauma—that is, how the trauma of genocide can be passed down through generations, impacting individuals who did not directly experience the atrocities themselves.

We will explore how this legacy continues to influence the lives of those who come after, shaping their experiences, beliefs, and relationships without their conscious awareness.

As we embark on this journey together, I hope this book will serve as a beacon of hope—a guiding light for those seeking to heal from past wounds and build a future filled with love, connection, and possibility. My sincerest belief is that by confronting the shadows of our past, we can pave the way for a brighter, more compassionate tomorrow—for ourselves, our families, and generations to come.

Thank you for joining me on this journey. May it be a source of inspiration, reflection, and transformation for us all.

INTRODUCTION

Welcome to "From Surviving to Thriving," a transformative exploration of how rebuilding relationships after trauma can lead to a life filled with purpose and connection.

Understanding the profound impact of relationships on our lives is paramount as we navigate the journey from surviving to thriving. As social beings, we are as wealthy as our relationships, and our lives truly travel at the speed of our connections with others.

Each connection, whether with ourselves or with others, enriches our human experience and shapes our journey through life. From the bonds formed within our families to the friendships forged in our communities, relationships provide us with a sense of belonging, support, and purpose.

In the aftermath of the 1994 Genocide against the Tutsi, countless individuals faced the unimaginable task of rebuilding their lives amidst the rubble of destruction and despair. But survival, as we will come to understand, is just the beginning of the journey.

"From Surviving to Thriving": Explaining the journey from merely surviving the trauma of genocide to actively working towards thriving in life.

This journey to thriving is a deeply personal and multifaceted process that unfolds over time.

It begins with recognizing that surviving alone is not enough and that true healing and growth require intentional effort and commitment. Through this journey, survivors confront the legacy of trauma, reclaim their sense of agency, and reimagine their futures with hope and possibility.

Before we proceed, I want to make sure you understand the concept of reclaiming agency, which will come up several times as you read.

"Reclaiming agency" in this context of healing refers to taking back control over one's own life, choices, and actions after experiencing trauma or adversity. It involves asserting one's autonomy, power, and sense of self in the face of challenges or circumstances that may have undermined or diminished it.

When individuals reclaim agency, they move from a state of feeling helpless or powerless to actively engaging in their own healing and growth process. This may involve setting boundaries, making empowered decisions, advocating for their needs, and taking proactive steps towards positive change.

Reclaiming agency is a profoundly empowering and transformative process that allows individuals to regain control and ownership over their lives. It involves recognizing and challenging any internalized beliefs or narratives that may have perpetuated feelings of victimhood or disempowerment and embracing a mindset of resilience, self-compassion, and empowerment.

Introduction

Ultimately, the reclaiming agency is about recognizing that despite the challenges and traumas one may have experienced, one still can shape one's own destiny, define one's own path, and create a future filled with hope, possibility, and purpose.

Reclaiming agency is akin to becoming the CEO and boss of one's own life. It involves asserting authority, making decisions, and taking action in alignment with one's values, goals, and aspirations. Just as a CEO directs the course of a company, reclaiming agency means taking charge of one's destiny and steering it toward healing, growth, and fulfillment. It's about recognizing that despite past challenges or traumas, one still holds the power to shape their present and future and to lead their life with purpose and autonomy.

It is a journey of self-discovery, resilience, and transformation, marked by moments of breakthrough and moments of setback, but ultimately leading towards a more vibrant and fulfilling life.

"Understanding the Impact": Delving into the profound and multifaceted effects of genocide trauma on individuals and families.

The impact of genocide trauma is far-reaching, extending beyond the immediate survivors to shape the lives of future generations. From the loss of loved ones to the erosion of cultural identity, the trauma of genocide leaves deep psychological, emotional, and relational scars that can persist for years, if not generations, to come. Understanding the multifaceted nature of this impact is essential for developing effective strategies for healing and recovery.

By exploring the interplay of biological, psychological, and social factors, we gain insight into the complex mechanisms through which trauma manifests and the pathways toward resilience and healing.

"The Importance of Healing": Emphasizing the significance of healing and rebuilding relationships as essential components of post-trauma recovery. Healing from genocide trauma is a holistic process that encompasses the physical, emotional, and spiritual dimensions of human experience. It involves not only addressing the symptoms of trauma but also nurturing a sense of wholeness and well-being.

Central to this process is rebuilding relationships—both with oneself and with others. By fostering connections based on trust, empathy, and mutual support, survivors create a supportive network as a foundation for healing and growth.

Through therapy, support groups, and other healing modalities, individuals can explore their trauma, process their emotions, and develop coping strategies for navigating the challenges of everyday life.

It's essential to recognize that healing does not happen automatically over time, as many tend to believe. It must be intentional and actively pursued through various therapeutic modalities, self-care practices, and support networks. If trauma is not correctly dealt with, it can manifest in multiple physical and psychological symptoms, leading to an increased risk of illness and premature death. As we are witnessing, many people are succumbing to mysterious diseases that are often rooted in unhealed trauma.

Introduction

In this book, we'll dive deeper into how to rebuild the basic relationships that form the foundation of our lives. You can think of all your relationships—past, present, and future—as falling into seven basic types. These categories help us understand the purpose, characteristics, and best practices for navigating each relationship successfully.

Each of these seven types of relationships serves a distinct purpose in our lives. From our relationship with our source, where we come from, which shapes our identity and sense of self, to our relationships with family members, spouses, friends, co-workers, and acquaintances, each connection uniquely shapes who we are and how we navigate the world.

One crucial aspect to consider is the concept of family, which is essentially formed through kinship, which forms the basis of our relationships. Kinship refers to relationships based on family ties through biological connections, but family can also be formed through marriage and adoption. Understanding the role of family in our lives can help us navigate relationship dynamics more effectively and appreciate the bonds we share with our loved ones.

Surviving the genocide may have impacted our ability to navigate these relationships fully. The trauma we've experienced can leave us feeling disconnected, distrustful, and uncertain of how to form meaningful connections with others.

In particular, the genocide may have removed those who are blood-related to us, leaving a void in our lives where kinship once existed but is no more.
This book will explore strategies for rebuilding our lives after that lack of kinship and finding new ways to connect with others.

Throughout the pages ahead, we'll discuss the purpose and characteristics of each relationship category and the best practices for successfully navigating them. We'll also explore how to prioritize our relationships to ensure we get the most out of our lives.

However, relationships aren't just limited to blood ties, marriage, or adoption. Many of our connections are formed through shared experiences or common interests. Whether it's friendships forged in school or bonds formed with colleagues in the workplace, these relationships contribute to our sense of belonging and fulfillment.

It's essential to recognize that relationships are dynamic—they evolve, grow, and sometimes end.

By understanding the different types of relationships and the factors that influence them, we can navigate our social interactions more effectively and lead more fulfilling lives.

So, let's embark on this journey together, exploring the complexities of human connection and discovering how to make the most of our relationships along the way.

I pray and believe this book will serve as a source of inspiration, reflection, and empowerment for all those who seek to heal from the wounds of the past and build a future filled with love, connection, and possibility.

CHAPTER 1

UNDERSTANDING
THE IMPACT OF TRAUMA ON YOUR RELATIONSHIPS

Before we talk about the impact of trauma on relationships, let's start by having a general and similar understanding of what trauma and relationships represent and why we should even care.

Trauma is a profound emotional and psychological response to distressing events that overwhelm an individual's ability to cope, often leaving a lasting impact on their psychological, emotional, and physical well-being. It is not just a momentary response to a crisis; trauma can linger, reshaping how individuals perceive the world, themselves, and their relationships. When we talk about trauma, it encompasses a wide range of experiences—from personal loss, accidents, and abuse to larger collective events such as wars, natural disasters, and genocides. These experiences leave indelible marks on individuals and communities, often manifesting in ways that extend far beyond the initial incident.

The 94 Genocide against the Tutsi in Rwanda stands as one of the most harrowing examples of collective trauma. Over the span of 100 days, over one million Tutsi were brutally murdered in an orchestrated campaign of violence, driven by deep-seated ethnic hatred.

The genocide left survivors with profound physical and emotional scars, not only from the horrific acts they witnessed but also from the unimaginable loss of loved ones, homes, and a sense of safety. This genocide represents a kind of trauma that is both individual and collective, affecting not only those who directly experienced it but also future generations, through the transmission of trauma and its effects on relationships and society as a whole.

The impact of the genocide on relationships is devastating. Trust, a fundamental element in any relationship, was shattered. Neighbors turned against neighbors, friends betrayed friends, and even within families, bonds were broken. The fear, suspicion, and pain carried by survivors made it difficult to rebuild these relationships in the aftermath. The trauma didn't just affect how individuals related to one another in the immediate sense; it also influenced the dynamics of future relationships, often manifesting as mistrust, anxiety, or emotional distance.

But trauma from such an atrocity does not only damage those who experienced it firsthand. It reverberates through generations, affecting the children and grandchildren of survivors. This phenomenon, known as intergenerational trauma, means that the pain, fear, and mistrust stemming from the genocide continue to affect relationships even decades later. Children born long after 1994 may struggle with the psychological and emotional weight of an event they never directly experienced, yet which has been passed down through family stories, behaviors, and even biological changes.

In this book, we delve deeply into the effects of trauma on relationships, using the 94 Genocide against the Tutsi as a primary case study. Through this lens, we explore how trauma disrupts trust, communication, and intimacy, and we examine the long road to healing and reconciliation. However, while our focus is on the 94 Genocide, the principles and insights drawn from this experience are applicable to various forms of trauma experienced by different individuals in different contexts. Whether the trauma is personal or collective, whether it stems from a singular event or prolonged suffering, the effects on relationships are profound and require understanding, compassion, and intentional efforts toward healing.

As we journey through this exploration, we aim to shed light on the complexities of trauma and offer pathways toward recovery, not just for survivors of the genocide but for anyone grappling with the aftermath of deeply traumatic experiences.

Coming back to relationships, Sonawat Rekha defines relationships as the connections and interactions between individuals, groups, objects, concepts, or entities. These connections can take various forms and exist in different contexts, such as personal, social, professional, familial, romantic, and more. Relationships play a fundamental role in shaping our lives and influencing our emotions, behaviors, and experiences.

Relationships are defined as bonds, links, connections, or bridges between people. They can be both intrapersonal and interpersonal. Intrapersonal relationships are those with ourselves, while interpersonal relationships are with other people. Relationships are kinships that can develop out of trust and common and/or shared experiences.

Relationships are so important that your private relationships are a matter of community and national concern. Your relationships may be private, but they are not personal.
As human beings, we are so interconnected that everything we do will eventually affect our family, our community, our nation, and the human race in general.

Even if your personal relationships are private, they have broader social impacts. For instance, studies have shown that healthy relationships and strong family units contribute positively to communities, while unhealthy relationships can lead to negative societal outcomes.

Humans are social beings.

We are social beings, and human life was designed to be interdependent. Humans are inherently social beings who thrive in interconnected relationships with others. Throughout history, humans have formed communities, families, and societies to collaborate, share resources, and support one another.

The difference between a good and a great human being is their ability to relate to others. If you want to successfully navigate each stage of your life, you are going to need a different group of people each time. You were born as a result of a relationship; your upbringing was all about relationships; school was all about relationships; and your professional life is all about relationships.

Your life travels at the speed of your relationships, which determines the pace at which you move through life. You are as wealthy as your relationships. Everything you need will come to you in one form or another through your relationships. You are where you are in life because of some sort of relationship, good or bad.

Relationships are so important that many sociologists believe that you are always four connections away from anyone on the planet. Any individual on the planet can reach anyone else through any four introductions or handshakes. It simply means that "you know someone, who knows someone, who knows someone, who knows someone to any human being." You are always four people away from any person.

John Guare, in the 1960s, popularized what was known as the six handshake rule or The theory of "six degrees of separation", a concept in social networks that states that any two people in the world can be connected to each other through a chain of acquaintances with no more than six intermediary connections. In other words, everyone is just a few steps away from anyone else in terms of social relationships.

Nowadays, globalization and advancements in communication, transportation, and technology have brought people and cultures closer together, making the world more interconnected and accessible, much like a small village.

In recent years, the rise of social media platforms and online networking has made it easier than ever to connect with individuals from different parts of the world. It is, therefore, imperative to note that it is no longer a matter of six handshakes but only four and/or less. In this social media era, you do not need to be connected to another individual through someone that you know; a simple like on a post will introduce two individuals who didn't know each other before.

As powerful as this interconnectedness is, being connected is one thing, but mastering relationships is what makes these relationships useful to you. The power does not lie in the connection between you and the people you connect with; the power lies in your mastery of navigating relationships successfully. The way you handle relationships will either make you or break you.

This being said, surviving the traumatic events of the 94 genocide against the Tutsi brings forth a myriad of challenges that profoundly affect our ability to navigate relationships effectively.

The 94 genocide against the Tutsi, deeply rooted in decades of instigated hatred, has left many grappling with profound trust issues. The betrayal and violence endured during the genocide shattered their fundamental belief in the goodness of humanity, making trust a scarce commodity guarded with vigilance. Rebuilding trust is a complex and arduous process that requires patience and understanding.
The shared trauma experienced by many survivors and those within their social circle further complicates this journey.

The aftermath of the genocide has created a landscape where suspicion and skepticism cloud many interactions, making genuine connection and intimacy challenging to achieve. Each relationship becomes a delicate dance between vulnerability and self-protection as many survivors navigate the complexities of trust in a world that has betrayed them.

After enduring trauma, it's very common for many to internalize a pervasive sense of insecurity, where the underlying belief emerges that "the world is not safe" and consequently, "I am not safe."

This deeply ingrained perception can lead to a profound sense of mistrust and wariness towards others and the world at large. However, amidst the darkness, it's essential to recognize that there are still many good people in the world, and the journey toward healing begins with reclaiming a sense of safety and security (we will explore this more in the coming pages).

Learning to trust again is a gradual and delicate process, akin to testing the waters cautiously rather than diving headfirst. By the way, trust is not a gift; it must be earned through testing over time. Do not fully trust what and who you have not tested first.

It's about approaching relationships and interactions with a circumspect mindset, allowing oneself the space and time needed to assess trustworthiness without rushing or forcing vulnerability prematurely. Through this gradual exploration, you begin to shift the internal narrative from one of fear and vulnerability to empowerment and agency.

The empowering message then becomes, "I can learn to keep myself as safe as possible," emphasizing the importance of self-preservation and self-care in the process of rebuilding trust.

This shift in perspective is liberating, as it acknowledges the individual's capacity to navigate the world with discernment and resilience.
True, connected relationships are indeed built on mutual trust, but this trust must first start from within, rooted in a deep sense of self-worth and agency.

By embracing this mindset, you embark on a journey of healing and transformation, gradually opening yourself up to the possibility of genuine connection and intimacy. Through patience, self-reflection, and a willingness to engage with vulnerability, you begin to cultivate relationships that are grounded in trust, reciprocity, and mutual respect. In doing so, you not only reclaim your sense of safety and security but also rediscover the beauty and resilience of the human spirit.

Communication, too, becomes a formidable hurdle as many still struggle to articulate the depth of their pain and horror. The genocide's trauma defies description, leaving many survivors feeling alone and misunderstood.

Fear of judgment further complicates communication, often leading to silence and suppression of emotions. Bridging this communication gap requires not only effective strategies like active listening and empathy but also a safe and supportive environment where we all feel validated and understood. Cultivating such an environment is essential for survivors to feel empowered to share their experiences and emotions openly, without fear of rejection or judgment.

Emotional scars from the 94 genocide against the Tusti can create a profound sense of detachment from oneself and others. In an attempt to shield themselves from further pain, many may withdraw emotionally, building walls around their hearts. This emotional distancing manifests in various ways within relationships, hindering intimacy and connection.

Overcoming this requires confronting and processing difficult emotions in a supportive environment where we can safely explore our vulnerabilities and fears. It involves dismantling the barriers erected to protect ourselves from further harm and rediscovering the capacity for genuine emotional connection and intimacy.

Intimacy, both physical and emotional, is profoundly impacted by the trauma of the 94 genocide. Intrusive memories may intrude upon moments of closeness, instilling fear of vulnerability and shame. Some may struggle to fully engage in intimate relationships, fearing re-traumatization and struggling to rebuild trust.

Addressing these intimacy issues requires patience, understanding, and a willingness to navigate the complexities of trauma and its impact on intimacy.

Trauma has a profound impact on our physiological and psychological responses, often leaving behind triggers that can evoke sensations reminiscent of the original traumatic event. These triggers have the power to transport us back to the trauma period, causing our bodies to react as if the threat were imminent once again. In such moments, it becomes imperative to attune to our body's signals, recognize the signs of distress, and respond with self-compassion and care. Returning to the present moment, pausing to breathe deeply, and approaching the experience with curiosity rather than fear can help us gain perspective and clarity.

By acknowledging that what we are feeling is a trigger and not the actual recurring trauma, we can begin to reclaim a sense of agency and control over our responses. Affirming to ourselves, "That was then, and this is now," serves as a powerful reminder of our capacity to navigate challenging experiences with resilience and strength. Creating a safe and supportive environment is essential for navigating triggers effectively.

Often, this involves seeking solace in a nurturing relationship characterized by understanding, empathy, and unconditional acceptance. Having a trusted confidant with whom we can openly discuss our experiences can provide validation and support, helping to alleviate feelings of isolation and distress.

Moreover, engaging in loving and intimate relationships stimulates the release of oxytocin, commonly known as the "bonding hormone," which promotes feelings of comfort and security, counteracting the physiological effects of adrenaline.

Adrenaline, also known as the "fight, flight, or freeze hormone," is often activated during triggering moments, preparing the body to respond to perceived threats. However, in the context of trauma triggers, this heightened state of alertness can exacerbate feelings of anxiety and distress, further reinforcing the need for soothing and supportive connections to restore a sense of calm and stability.

In moments of triggering, prioritizing safety and self-care is paramount. By cultivating a compassionate and nurturing inner dialogue, seeking support from trusted individuals, and fostering loving connections, we can mitigate the impact of triggers and reclaim a sense of stability and well-being. Through these intentional practices, we empower ourselves to navigate the complexities of trauma with grace and resilience, embracing the healing journey with courage and compassion.

Unresolved anger and hostility are common responses to trauma, often leading to strained relationships with family, friends, and romantic partners. It is normal for survivors to struggle with overwhelming feelings of rage and resentment towards those who perpetrated or enabled the violence, as well as towards themselves for surviving when others did not. Addressing these intense emotions requires a multifaceted approach that includes awareness, emotional regulation skills, and trauma processing techniques. It involves acknowledging and validating the validity of these emotions while also exploring healthy ways of expressing and processing them.

You may experience conflicting impulses regarding your relationships, oscillating between seeking connection & guarding your independence. Striking a balance requires a supportive environment that encourages healthy interdependence while respecting individual autonomy.

Navigating these dynamics involves understanding and validating your unique needs and personal coping mechanisms, fostering a sense of safety and security in your relationships.

It entails creating space for us to explore our identities and desires within the context of our relationships, empowering us to navigate the complexities of intimacy and connection.

The loss of family members fractures familial relationships, leaving many grappling with grief and resentment. Rebuilding family dynamics necessitates open communication, empathy, and creating new traditions that honor the memory of those lost. It also requires addressing feelings of anger and betrayal towards those who were complicit in the genocide against Tutsi or failed to protect our loved ones. This process is fraught with challenges and requires patience, understanding, and a willingness to confront difficult emotions together as a nation.

Many survivors can develop coping mechanisms, such as substance abuse, to navigate their pain, which can interfere with healthy relationship functioning. Addressing these coping patterns requires professional assistance and support to foster resilience and healing. It entails creating a safe space where they feel empowered to confront their emotions and develop healthier coping strategies. This may involve therapy, support groups, and other forms of professional assistance to help them identify and address harmful coping patterns while fostering resilience and healing.

In summary, the trauma of the 94 genocide against the Tutsi casts a long shadow over many survivors' relationships, shaping their perceptions, behaviors, and interactions in profound ways.

Overcoming these challenges requires a comprehensive and compassionate approach that addresses the multidimensional nature of our experiences, fostering healing and resilience on our journey toward recovery. It entails creating a supportive environment where we all feel empowered to confront our trauma and navigate the complexities of intimacy, trust, and communication within our relationships.

Additionally, it is crucial to acknowledge the broader societal context in which we are living, where the focus on rebuilding the nation's physical infrastructure may have overshadowed the need for internal healing and support.

The notion of healing through the expression of pain is very problematic in Rwandans because it confronts formidable cultural barriers. Cultural proverbs like "Ntago ugomba kwimena inda" (you should not open up your guts) and "Amarira y'umugabo atemba ajya mu nda" (tears of men go into the guts) reflect a belief that emotions should be contained within, hidden from view.

However, this cultural norm reveals a deeper truth: the suppression of pain only serves to amplify suffering, manifesting in physical impairments and unseen illnesses. Indeed, the body holds onto pain, absorbing it like a sponge until it seeps into every fiber of our being, wreaking havoc on our physical and emotional well-being. The reluctance to share our pain, to open up and release its grip, only perpetuates this cycle of internalized suffering. It is no wonder, then, that many individuals succumb to illnesses that were once unseen, their bodies bearing the burden of unexpressed grief and trauma.

Indeed, when we suppress our pain and fail to address our emotional wounds, the consequences can manifest in various forms of illness. The impact is profound and extends beyond just emotional distress.

Physiologically, the stress of unresolved trauma can cause serious damage to our bodies, leading to inflammation and weakening our immune systems. Chronic stress, often a result of unprocessed trauma, has been linked to numerous health issues, including heart disease and hypertension.

Furthermore, the use of alcohol and substances to numb emotional pain can lead to addiction and exacerbate mental health struggles. The temporary relief these substances provide often masks the underlying issues, trapping individuals in a cycle of dependency and worsening their overall well-being.

Mentally, unaddressed trauma can contribute to the development of depression and anxiety disorders. The weight of unresolved pain can become unbearable, leading to feelings of hopelessness and despair. In severe cases, individuals may contemplate or even attempt suicide as a means of escape from their suffering.

Therefore, it becomes evident that the ramifications of unhealed trauma extend far beyond the emotional realm, permeating into every aspect of our health and well-being. It underscores the urgent need for proactive measures to address and heal from the scars of our past experiences.

Yet, despite these cultural barriers, there exists a profound strength in vulnerability, a resilience born of the willingness to confront our pain head-on.

Sharing your struggles is not a sign of weakness but a testament to your courage and determination to heal. It is a declaration of your humanity, a recognition that you are not meant to carry your burdens alone. By embracing your pain by allowing yourself to be seen and heard, you create space for healing and transformation to take root.

The significance of vocalizing our experiences lies in their transformative power. It shifts the nebulous discomfort swirling within our guts into the realm of language, where clarity and understanding await.

By engaging the language center of our brain, we tap into our frontal cortex—the seat of our executive functions—empowering ourselves to offer reassurance, find calm amidst chaos, and embark on the journey of problem-solving. That is why, when you go see a psychologist, you may be healed just by talking; it is so powerful.

Let me talk a bit about this: tears, often regarded as the silent language of the soul, carry the weight of unspoken pain and unexpressed emotions. When words fail us, when the depth of our suffering defies expression, tears become our voice, conveying the raw intensity of our inner turmoil. In their silent descent, tears speak volumes, articulating the unspoken anguish that weighs heavy on our hearts. But beyond their symbolic significance, tears serve as a powerful pathway to healing.

They are the cathartic release valve through which pent-up emotions find expression. Each tear shed is a step towards emotional liberation, a shedding of the burdens that threaten to consume us from within.

In the gentle cascade of tears, we find solace, a reprieve from the relentless grip of pain. Moreover, tears hold within them the seeds of transformation.

Tears nourish the seeds of resilience and hope as they moisten the arid landscape of our souls, fostering new growth amidst the rubble of our shattered dreams. They cleanse the wounds of our past, washing away the stains of sorrow and regret and paving the way for renewal and rebirth. In embracing our tears, we embrace the full spectrum of our humanity—the moments of joy, the depths of despair, and everything in between. We honor the sacredness of our pain and acknowledge its role in shaping who we are. In doing so, we open ourselves to the possibility of healing, allowing tears to serve as the gentle rain that nourishes the garden of our souls, coaxing forth the blossoms of wholeness and restoration.

The depth and magnitude of our suffering demand a profound reevaluation of the beliefs anchoring us in our pain. Our trauma is not merely a surface wound; it runs deep, permeating every aspect of our being and shaping the very fabric of our reality.

In confronting the enormity of our suffering, we face the stark reality that some of the beliefs we once held dear may no longer serve us.

We must be willing to challenge the narratives that keep us tethered to our past to interrogate the assumptions that have become ingrained in our collective consciousness. Beliefs that once provided comfort, and security may now act as barriers to our healing, perpetuating cycles of suffering and stagnation. We can create space for new truths to emerge by shedding these outdated beliefs and unlearning what we thought we knew. This process of introspection and reevaluation is not easy; it requires courage and humility to confront the deeply ingrained beliefs that have shaped our identities and worldviews. Yet, it is also a journey of liberation, a pathway to reclaiming agency and authorship over our own lives. As we challenge the limiting beliefs that bind us, we open ourselves to the possibility of transformation, embracing a new way of being rooted in resilience, strength, and hope.

For believers, this act of vocalization takes on added depth and meaning as we weave our words into prayers, forging a sacred connection with God.
Through prayer, we transcend the confines of our earthly existence, reaching out to God for guidance and solace in distress.

As we lift our voices in prayer, we invite the presence of the Comforter, the Spirit of peace, into our lives, finding refuge in His embrace.

However, as you know, in our country, which has suffered unspeakable loss, the general suffering has remained silent and has rarely been expressed. Yet, in the act of speaking our truth, healing begins to take root. Only by giving voice to our grief can we release its grip on our hearts, allowing the process of mourning to pave the way for acceptance and hope to flourish.

In the tapestry of Rwanda's collective trauma, the absence of spoken pain served as a barrier to healing, perpetuating a cycle of suffering and silence. Yet, confronting the silence with courage and compassion opens the door to healing and transformation. Through the alchemy of expression, we reclaim our voices, honor our losses, and ultimately find redemption by embracing acceptance and hope.

But, just like tending to a physical wound requires careful attention and treatment, emotional wounds demand similar care and support.

However, unlike physical wounds that can be addressed by medical professionals in sterile environments, emotional healing hinges on empathy, understanding, and genuine human connection.

Creating a safe space for emotional healing extends beyond the presence of therapists or counselors; it necessitates individuals who can listen without judgment and offer unwavering compassion and support.

These empathic listeners, pivotal in the healing journey, provide a nonjudgmental environment where individuals can freely share their stories of pain and trauma. In this sanctuary of understanding, individuals can express their emotions without fear, secure in the knowledge that they will be met with empathy and validation.

Empathic listeners refrain from imposing their own experiences or attempting to "fix" the situation; instead, they offer a compassionate presence that allows the storyteller to feel heard and affirmed.

To foster a community of trained listeners, we must begin by cultivating our own skills as effective listeners. This entails actively listening, validating emotions, and supporting without overshadowing the speaker's experiences. It's crucial to recognize that each person's suffering is unique and valid, regardless of whether their pain seems comparable to our own or someone else's.

By refining these listening skills, we can establish safe havens within our communities where individuals feel empowered to share their stories and seek support as they embark on their journey toward healing.

Despite the amazing, visible progress Rwanda has made in the aftermath of the genocide, studies show that Rwandans are not as happy as they could be. Foreigners often perceive Rwandans as cold or distant, failing to understand the deep scars left by the 94 genocide against the Tutsi and its ongoing impact on mental health.

IMPACT OF TRAUMA

According to the Rwanda Biometric Center (RBC), one in five Rwandans exhibits at least one sign of mental health issues, highlighting the urgent need for greater awareness, understanding, and support for us all as we continue our journey towards healing and recovery.

Yes, surviving traumatic events such as the 1994 genocide against the Tutsi presents many challenges that can hinder our ability to navigate relationships effectively. However, I firmly believe that despite these obstacles, healing, wholeness, and rebuilding our internal beings and relationships are possible.

We possess an inherent resilience that enables us to overcome adversity and emerge stronger. By confronting our trauma, acknowledging its impact on our lives, and seeking support and healing, we can chart a path toward personal and collective transformation. In doing so, we not only reclaim our sense of self but also contribute to our nation's greater healing and advancement.

This journey of healing and self-discovery is integral to our individual and collective growth, laying the foundation for a future characterized by resilience, compassion, and unity.

As we embark on this journey of healing and renewal, it becomes imperative to delve deeper into the process of rebuilding our identity and self-image. The aftermath of trauma often leaves many grappling with questions of who they are and where they belong in the world.

In the next chapter, we will explore how the experiences of the 94 genocide against the Tutsi have shaped our sense of self. We will examine the challenges we face in reclaiming our true identity and cultivating a positive self-image. By understanding the complexities of this process, we can take meaningful steps towards rediscovering our identity, embracing who we truly are, and accepting our worth as individuals.

Through this journey of self-discovery, we can begin to heal the wounds of the past and forge a path toward a brighter and more fulfilling future.

CHAPTER 2

REBUILDING YOUR TRUE IDENTITY AND SELF-IMAGE

As we embark on the journey from surviving to thriving, with a keen focus on rebuilding relationships, it's imperative to recognize the profound impact of our identity on the dynamics of our relationships.

Before delving into the depths of our true identity, we must first grasp how our sense of self influences our interactions with others. Indeed, your identity, or the relationship with yourself, is the cornerstone of all other relationships. It serves as the foundation upon which every interaction is built, shaping the way you relate to others and the world around you.

To comprehend the principles of cultivating healthy relationships, we must devote attention to the concept of self-mastery—the art of fostering a harmonious relationship with ourselves. Much like a mirror reflects your physical appearance, relationships act as mirrors of your innermost being. Each interaction serves as a reflection of your thoughts, emotions, values, and desires.

This concept is supported by the Sociometer Theory proposed by social psychologists Leary and Baumeister, which suggests that individuals' self-esteem is an internal measure for assessing social acceptance and standing.

IDENTITY

Your inner being is the innermost aspect of your thoughts, emotions, feelings, moods, beliefs, values, desires, motivations, and moral compass.

It encompasses the deepest aspects of your psyche that shape your perception of yourself and the world. Your inner being acts as a magnet, drawing like-minded individuals into your orbit and guiding your connections with others. Your intrinsic sense of self-worth will significantly shape your approach to initiating, nurturing, and sustaining relationships, exerting a profound influence on your actions and decisions.

Indeed, birds of a feather flock together as shared values and beliefs form the bedrock of meaningful relationships.

Moreover, every relationship in your life serves a purpose, whether to enhance your strengths or shed light on your weak areas for growth. Yes, some relationships in your life are there to strengthen and build upon the good aspects within you, while others highlight areas that need change. Many relationships are a tool for revealing the issues we need to address and refine. Recurring relationship patterns or conflicts provide invaluable opportunities for introspection and personal development. Rather than seeking to change others, it's essential to focus on transforming oneself internally, using relationships as a mirror to illuminate areas needing refinement.

John Bowlby's attachment theory further underscores the intricate link between early experiences and adult relationship dynamics.

Our internal representations of attachment forged in childhood significantly influence our connections with others in adulthood, shaping our expectations, behaviors, and responses within relationships.

This theory explores how early experiences with caregivers shape an individual's internal working models of relationships. At its core, your inner being is a construct of self-perception—a narrative woven from your beliefs, experiences, and societal influences. It reflects who you are and how you perceive yourself and your place in the world.

This self-perception is a potent force, shaping not just your relationships but your entire life trajectory, predicting the outcomes you manifest and the person you ultimately become. Understanding and nurturing your relationship with yourself is paramount, as it sets the stage for cultivating meaningful connections with others. By embracing your inner being and aligning it with your authentic self, you pave the way for profound personal growth, fulfilling relationships, and a life of purpose and authenticity.

The journey to regain your true identity and thrive begins with recognizing that your self-perception is not fixed or immutable but rather a dynamic and evolving narrative shaped by your experiences, beliefs, and interactions.

By acknowledging the influence of societal norms, cultural values, and personal experiences on your sense of self, you can unravel the layers of conditioning that have shaped your identity. As you peel back these layers, you may uncover insecurities, fears, and doubts that have prevented you from embracing your true essence. Yet, amidst these challenges lie moments of strength, resilience, and triumph that affirm your innate worth and potential.

Through introspection and self-awareness, you can challenge limiting beliefs and embrace empowering truths about yourself, paving the way for a more authentic and aligned sense of self.

IDENTITY

This journey of self-discovery is not always easy, requiring courage, vulnerability, and perseverance. Yet, as you delve deeper into your inner being, you will uncover hidden depths of strength, wisdom, and resilience that have always been within you.

By aligning your inner narrative with your authentic truth, you empower yourself to step into the fullness of who you are and create a life that reflects your deepest desires and highest aspirations.

In essence, the journey to regain your true identity and thrive is a process of self-liberation—a journey of reclaiming your power, agency, and autonomy. It is a journey of self-acceptance, self-love, and self-empowerment. This journey begins within and radiates outward, transforming not only your relationship with yourself but also your relationships with others and the world around you.

So embrace this journey with an open heart and a courageous spirit, for within you lies the power to rewrite your story and create a life of purpose, passion, and fulfillment.

WHAT IS YOUR IDENTITY?

Let's delve deeper into identity and its significance in shaping our lives.

The English word "identity" stems from the verb "identify," which involves recognizing or establishing someone or something as unique from others. Essentially, your identity encompasses the essence of who you are, setting you apart from everyone on the planet. It includes many factors, including your unique talents, abilities, personalities, experiences, values, and, most importantly, the trajectory of your life.

Albert Bandura, a prominent psychologist known for his social cognitive theory, offered a profound definition of identity. He described it as "an internal working model of oneself that integrates one's personal characteristics, values, and goals," highlighting the complex interplay of internal perceptions and external influences. This definition underscores the notion that our identity is not static but dynamic, shaped by our experiences, relationships, and social environment. At the core of identity lies our self-perception—an internal model of ourselves that emerges when all facades are stripped away. It encompasses our thoughts, feelings, attitudes, and behaviors when alone, offering a glimpse into our true essence. This self-perception forms the foundation of our identity, serving as a subconscious image that shapes how we view ourselves and interact with the world.

Therefore, identity is a multifaceted construct encompassing a rich tapestry of characteristics, beliefs, values, attitudes, and experiences. It is an internal reflection of who we are and an external projection of how others perceive us—a dynamic interplay influenced by many factors.

IDENTITY

From our genetic predispositions and family backgrounds to cultural influences and personal experiences, every aspect of our identity is shaped by a unique blend of elements.

It serves as the lens through which we interpret ourselves and navigate the complexities of the world around us. Indeed, identity permeates every facet of our lives, from our relationships and career paths to our aspirations and responses to challenges. It guides our interactions with others, shaping the formation of friendships, romantic partnerships, and community engagements.

Moreover, our identity holds profound personal significance, serving as a source of pride, heritage, and individuality. Embracing our identity fosters self-acceptance and authenticity, allowing us to honor our past while embracing our future. Identity is not merely a static construct but a dynamic force that shapes our perceptions, behaviors, and life trajectories.

We lay the groundwork for personal growth, fulfillment, and well being by cultivating a positive and cohesive sense of identity. In this chapter, we embark on a journey of self-discovery, exploring the intricacies of identity and its profound impact on our quest to thrive in the aftermath of adversity. We delve into reconnecting with our origins, overcoming identity crisis, and fostering self-acceptance and self-love. Through introspection and exploration, we seek to unravel the layers of our identity and embrace our true essence, paving the way for a life of authenticity, purpose, and fulfillment.

THE POWER OF SELF-PERCEPTION

As defined by prominent social psychologists Elliot Aronson, Timothy D. Wilson, and Robin M. Akert, self-perception is the internal view of oneself, encompassing abilities, qualities, and characteristics. Various factors influence it, including experiences, relationships, and cultural background. Yet, its impact extends far beyond mere self-image; it shapes our goals, motivation, and response to challenges.

Henry Ford, the American industrialist and founder of the Ford Motor Company, was a visionary industrialist who revolutionized the automobile industry and transformed modern manufacturing is the father of this famous adage: "If you believe you can, you are right; if you believe you can't, you are not wrong either." This succinctly illustrates the profound influence of self-perception on actions and outcomes. Those with a positive self-perception set ambitious goals and persevere in facing obstacles. Conversely, a negative self-perception can become a self-fulfilling prophecy, leading to resignation and missed opportunities.

The famous basketball player Michael Jordan's journey epitomizes the power of self-belief. Despite setbacks, his unwavering confidence propelled him to greatness.

His belief in continuous improvement and resilience enabled him to overcome challenges and achieve remarkable success. Jordan's mindset wasn't just about winning games; it was a fundamental belief in his capacity to excel, on and off the court. Indeed, mindset shapes outcomes. A Harvard Business School study underscores this, revealing that employees with a growth mindset are more innovative. Researchers discovered that compared to people with fixed mindsets,

IDENTITY

those with growth mindsets were 65 percent more likely to innovate because they were more likely to be adaptable and creative.

In life, attitude reigns supreme. Lions, not the fastest, wisest, or strongest, command the jungle due to their attitude. Similarly, our self-perception dictates our trajectory. It determines whether we soar to new heights or remain grounded. How we see ourselves is a potent force, influencing thoughts, words, and actions and ultimately shaping our reality.

SELF PERCEPTION VS. IDENTITY

Your self-perception, the internal image you hold of yourself, is the cornerstone of your life. As the wise King Solomon once noted, "As a man thinketh in his heart, so is he." This profound insight underscores the immense power of your thoughts and beliefs in shaping your reality. Contrary to popular belief, your self-perception is not merely a reflection of external opinions or circumstances. It is the most profound, subconscious image of who you believe yourself to be, influencing every aspect of your existence.

Regardless of your background, upbringing, or innate talents, your self-perception ultimately determines the trajectory of your life.

Your self-perception is not static but is constantly evolving, shaped by many factors such as your early experiences, feedback from others, social comparisons, successes, and failures. It is deeply intertwined with your belief system, the pattern of thoughts that dictate how you view yourself and the world around you. The subconscious mind, the seat of all power, is crucial in shaping your self-perception.

As Joseph Murphy elucidates in his seminal work "The Power of Your Subconscious Mind," your subconscious mind profoundly influences your thoughts, feelings, and behaviors. Reprogramming your subconscious mind is essential if you seek to change your self-perception and belief systems, requiring self-awareness, reflection, and positive self-talk.

The transformative potential of self-perception is vividly illustrated in the life of my late mentor, Dr. Myles Munroe, a Bahamian-born individual who overcame profound challenges to become a beacon of inspiration and empowerment. As a young boy in the Bahamas, Dr. Munroe faced academic struggles and endured hurtful labels from his racist teachers, who dismissed him and his classmates as incapable black men compared to retarded monkeys.

However, his life took a remarkable turn when his mother shared a profound truth: the power to succeed resides within oneself. Driven by his mother's empowering words, Dr. Munroe immersed himself in the scriptures, particularly *Ephesians 3:20*, which emphasizes the boundless potential within each individual.

Through relentless repetition and affirmation, he internalized the belief that the power to achieve greatness lay within him. This newfound self-belief catalyzed a remarkable transformation in Dr. Munroe's life.

Despite his early academic setbacks, he emerged as a stellar student, achieving academic excellence and setting his sights on a future filled with purpose and possibility. Dr. Munroe's journey exemplifies the transformative power of self-perception. By embracing a positive and empowering view of himself, he transcended the limitations imposed by others and charted a path to extraordinary success. His story serves as a potent reminder that what you believe about yourself has the power to shape your reality.

By cultivating a positive self-perception and embracing your inherent potential, you can overcome obstacles, achieve your goals, and create a life of purpose and fulfillment.

Essentially, what you believe about yourself is infinitely more powerful than external opinions or circumstances. Your self-perception shapes your thoughts, feelings, behaviors, and outcomes, influencing how you navigate challenges, pursue goals, and interact with the world. By cultivating a positive and empowering self-perception, you unlock your full potential and create the life you envision.

Indeed, your perception of yourself shapes your reality. When you believe in your abilities, potential, and worth, you pave the way for success and fulfillment. Conversely, doubts or negative beliefs about yourself can limit your potential and hinder your progress. Your self-perception acts as a self-fulfilling prophecy, influencing your thoughts, actions, and outcomes.

By cultivating a positive and empowering self-perception, you unlock the door to endless possibilities and set yourself on a path to realizing your dreams.

HOW YOUR IDENTITY IS SHAPED

Understanding the intricate processes that shape our identity requires a deep dive into the interconnected realms of self-perception, belief systems, and the information we internalize from various sources. At the core of our identity lies our self-perception—the lens through which we view ourselves and our place in the world.

This self-perception, in turn, is shaped by our belief system—a complex network of values, attitudes, and assumptions that guide our thoughts, behaviors, and decision-making processes. However, the foundation of our belief system is built upon the information we hold to be true, which is acquired from many sources throughout our lives. From the earliest stages of development, we are influenced by the information we receive from those around us.

Our parents, siblings, relatives, and caregivers play a crucial role in shaping our beliefs about ourselves and the world. Their words, actions, and behaviors serve as powerful models that inform our understanding of reality. Additionally, our interactions with peers, teachers, mentors, and authority figures contribute to the construction of our belief system. Positive reinforcement, encouragement, and validation can bolster our self-esteem and confidence, while criticism, neglect, and abuse can sow seeds of doubt and insecurity.

Furthermore, the media, including television, movies, books, and social media platforms, also play a significant role in shaping our beliefs and perceptions. These influential sources of information often portray idealized images of beauty, success, and happiness, which can distort our perceptions of reality and create unrealistic expectations.

Moreover, cultural norms, societal values, and religious teachings further contribute to the formation of our belief system, dictating what is considered acceptable or taboo within our communities.

The impact of our belief system extends beyond individual perceptions to societal structures and power dynamics.

IDENTITY

Note that historical events, such as slavery, colonization, and genocide, have left lasting imprints on collective consciousness, shaping the beliefs and attitudes of entire populations.

The dehumanization of marginalized groups, such as African Americans, Indigenous peoples, and other ethnic minorities (we will expand more on this down the lines) has perpetuated systems of oppression and inequality, reinforcing deeply ingrained stereotypes and prejudices.

Did you know that for example, the legacy of slavery in the United States of America continues to reverberate through generations, with systemic racism and institutionalized discrimination continuing to shape the lived experiences of African Americans?

Glenn C. Loury, a prominent scholar, elucidates how the belief in the inferiority of black individuals justified centuries of exploitation, oppression, and violence. This deeply entrenched belief system has profound implications for the self-perception and identity of African Americans (Black Americans), contributing to feelings of inadequacy, inferiority, and self-doubt.

Moreover, the pervasive impact of systemic inequality is evident in various aspects of life, including education, healthcare, employment, and criminal justice. Despite progress towards racial equality, disparities persist, perpetuating cycles of poverty, marginalization, and social exclusion. Karuna Meda highlights the enduring legacy of slavery in contemporary society, underscoring the need for systemic change and collective action to dismantle structural barriers and promote equity and justice for all.

Our identity is shaped by a complex interplay of self-perception, belief systems, and external influences, including the information we internalize from our social environment. By critically examining the sources of our beliefs and challenging ingrained stereotypes and prejudices, we can cultivate a more inclusive, empathetic, and authentic sense of self and contribute to creating a more equitable and just society for future generations.

We should pay attention here because each aspect of the interconnected journey from information to identity holds profound implications for how we perceive ourselves and navigate the world around us.

The process begins with the information we receive, which serves as the building blocks of our belief system. As we absorb information from various sources, including family, friends, educators, and societal influences, we internalize certain ideas about ourselves and the world.

However, the accuracy and reliability of this information can vary widely, leading to discrepancies in our belief systems. For many individuals, the information they receive about themselves is deeply intertwined with their cultural heritage, familial upbringing, and social environment. In contexts where prejudice, discrimination, and historical trauma prevail, such as our case in Rwanda, misinformation and dehumanizing narratives have devastating consequences.

The deliberate propagation of harmful stereotypes and derogatory labels, such as "snakes" and "cockroaches," served to strip away the Tutsi people's humanity and erode their sense of identity.

Moreover, the individuals and institutions entrusted with shaping our perceptions of ourselves may themselves be influenced by flawed ideologies and limited understanding. Parents, caregivers, and educators have inadvertently perpetuated harmful narratives or reinforced outdated identity beliefs.

Even political leaders and public figures, as President Kagame reflected on the enduring legacy of colonial mentality in Africa, can shape collective perceptions and attitudes through their rhetoric and policies.

President Kagame's message, delivered on the official Presidency Twitter account by Urugwiro Village on October 27, 2017, at 11:02 PM, encapsulates the profound impact of historical narratives on contemporary identity formation. He stated, "We have continued to be slaves; the colonial mentality still drives our thinking." This acknowledgment underscores the enduring influence of colonialism on African societies and highlights the ongoing struggle to reclaim authentic identities free from external imposition. It is a reminder that although African countries have gained political independence, they still grapple with colonialism's psychological and cultural legacy. Colonial mentality is the belief that Africans are inferior to Europeans and that European culture and values are superior to African culture.

This still manifests in so many ways. Africans continue to downplay their own accomplishments and put down their culture. Many Africans still believe that European ideas and values matter more than theirs.

Some Africans believe they depend on Europeans for their development and progress, which is why there are still high levels of foreign aid.

Understanding the complexities of identity formation requires a critical examination of the sources of our beliefs and perceptions. This involves asking probing questions about who told us who we are and what motivations or biases may have shaped their narratives. It also entails acknowledging the limitations of our own perspectives and recognizing that our understanding of ourselves is subject to continual refinement and evolution.

Dr. Myles Munroe's transformative journey serves as a poignant reminder of the power of self-perception and the potential for personal growth and empowerment. Despite facing adversity and internalizing negative messages about his abilities, Dr. Munroe's mother provided him with a powerful counter-narrative rooted in faith and self-belief. By internalizing the empowering message that the power to achieve greatness resided within him, Dr. Munroe was able to overcome his academic struggles and chart a path to success and fulfillment. My personal life is the fruit of this mindset shift in his life.

However, the journey towards self-discovery and identity correction is not without its challenges. It requires a willingness to confront entrenched beliefs, challenge societal norms, and embrace discomfort and uncertainty. Moreover, it demands a commitment to seeking out accurate and reliable sources of information that affirm and validate our true worth and potential.

Ultimately, correcting our identity begins with reclaiming agency over our own narratives and rejecting the falsehoods and distortions that have been imposed upon us.

It involves cultivating a deep sense of self-awareness, self-compassion, and resilience in the face of adversity. By embracing our inherent worth and recognizing the inherent dignity of others, we can transcend the limitations of false perceptions and forge a path toward authenticity, fulfillment, and belonging.

IDENTITY

As we delve deeper into the journey of self-discovery, we recognize the significance of reconnecting with our origins and understanding the factors that have shaped our identity. For many of us, our identity is intricately tied to our cultural heritage, family background, and personal experiences. Reconnecting with these roots allows us to gain a deeper understanding of who we are and where we come from. However, the process of reconnecting with our origins can be complex, especially for those who have experienced trauma or loss.

For survivors of genocide, war, or displacement, the journey of reconnecting with our identity will involve confronting painful memories and navigating feelings of grief, anger, and loss. It requires courage, emotional resilience, support from loved ones and mental health professionals, and a willingness to confront the past in order to move forward.

In addition to reconnecting with our origins, overcoming identity crises is an essential aspect of the journey toward self-acceptance and self love. Identity crises may arise when we feel disconnected from our sense of self, unsure of who we are or where we belong. These crises can be triggered by major life transitions, such as changes in relationships, careers, or personal beliefs. Reconnecting with our origins is a process of introspection and exploration, delving into our past to uncover the threads that weave the fabric of our identity. It involves revisiting cherished memories, honoring ancestral traditions, and embracing cultural heritage.

Through this journey, we not only gain a deeper appreciation for our roots but also reclaim a sense of belonging and purpose.

For survivors of trauma, the journey of reconnecting with their identity may also entail confronting difficult truths and reconciling with the past. It requires confronting painful memories and acknowledging the impact of past experiences on their sense of self. Yet, it is through this process of acknowledgment and acceptance that healing can begin. As we navigate this journey, it's essential to recognize that healing is not a linear process. There will be moments of struggle and setback, but also moments of growth and transformation. It's important to be patient and compassionate with ourselves, allowing ourselves the time and space needed to heal.

In addition to individual healing, community support plays a crucial role in the process of reconnecting with our identity. Sharing our stories, experiences, and struggles with others who have walked similar paths can provide validation, understanding, and solidarity. It fosters a sense of community and belonging, reminding us that we are not alone in our journey. Ultimately, the journey of reconnecting with our origins is a deeply personal and transformative experience. It requires courage, resilience, and self-reflection, but it also offers the opportunity for growth, healing, and self-discovery. As we embrace our roots and honor our heritage, we not only reconnect with our identity but also pave the way for a more authentic and fulfilling life.

Before I go further, let me remind you that your past does not define you today. It is essential to recognize that the information you were given about yourself may not accurately reflect who you truly are. Where you were born does not define how far you can go; your place of birth or upbringing does not determine your potential and success.

Your past mistakes do not define your present or future; you can learn from them and make different choices moving forward.

So many people are products of their past and mess up their present and future. Of course, your past plays a significant role in where you are today and who you will become tomorrow, but your origin should only be there to show your starting point, and it is essential to recognize and understand where you come from. But your origin is to allow you to set up your future and not be limited by it. Believing misinformation about yourself can lead to a distorted self-perception and hinder personal growth. Questioning and challenging these false narratives to develop a more authentic understanding of yourself is crucial.

Before discussing correcting your identity, let's look at the devastating effects of wrong perception and identity.

Devastating effects of wrong self-identity:

a. <u>Suicide and self-harm</u>

Different scientific research and statistics have shown that individuals with identity disturbance or an unstable sense of self are more likely to experience suicidal thoughts and harm themselves. This is because a lack of clear identity can lead to feelings of hopelessness, worthlessness, and disconnection from others.

The Journal of Abnormal Psychology's study in 2019 of 1,000 adolescents found that those with identity disturbance were 4.5 times more likely to experience suicidal ideation than those without identity disturbance.

The Journal of Clinical Psychiatry's study in 2020 of 2,000 adults found that those with identity disturbance were 2.5 times more likely to experience suicidal ideation than those without identity disturbance (Jones et al., 2020).

It is vital to know your true identity and be sure about it for yourself and those who will come after you. You need to be grounded and understand your true self.

Self-harm is not just limited to physical harm because the wrong identity may be the origin of your failure in business or everything else you are involved in. You will sabotage your own success if you have a false self-perception.

    b.   <u>Your belief system shapes your worldview and values</u>

When you form a belief about a group of people, you start to see them through that belief's lens. We don't see others as they are but see them according to who we are and what we believe about ourselves.

People who kill others must first see them as non-humans to ease their conscience about what they are doing. The other way is that their humanity has been crushed, and they have been equated to animals to the extent that they don't think they are humans, so they do not act as humans but as barbarians.

Researchers Landry, Orr, and Mere explain that the key factor in the Holocaust was dehumanization. Nazi propagandists made the Jews seem like they were highly capable of planning and intentionality but also that they had a subhuman moral character. The propagandists wanted to demonize the Jews so that they could justify killing them in large numbers. Perpetrators of all kinds often think of their victims as mindless barbarians, and this was also true during the Holocaust.

IDENTITY

Susan Optow notes, "Dehumanization is a psychological process whereby opponents view each other as less than human and thus not deserving of moral consideration.

Jews in the eyes of Nazis and Tutsis in the eyes of extremist Hutus (in the 94 Genocide against Tutsis in Rwanda) are but two examples. Protracted conflict strains relationships and makes it difficult for parties to recognize that they are part of a shared human community. Such conditions often lead to intense hatred and alienation among conflicting parties. The more severe the conflict, the more the psychological distance between groups will widen. Eventually, this can result in moral exclusion. Those excluded are typically viewed as inferior, evil, or criminal"

You are a product of your beliefs; what you think about yourself determines your feelings about others. This is why you need to clearly understand what you believe, because it shapes who you think you are and will affect all your relationships.

Most of the problems you see around result from the intrapersonal relationship. You could have caused many problems for yourself and those around you because of a poor understanding of who you are.

You also could have denied the world the gifts you were sent to give because of your poor self-perception. Understanding who you truly are and your true identity is essential to living a worthy life.

To understand identity, first, you must understand your belief system and self-conception and decide whether you have the right kind of information. Many people are not who they are supposed to be because they have the wrong information about themselves, which has affected everything about them.

So, who are you? Who do you think you are? Who told you who you are? Do you even know who you truly are?

CORRECTING YOUR SELF-IDENTITY

As discussed, distorted self-identity is a product of the wrong information you have believed to be true about yourself. The only way to correct your self-identity is by finding accurate information about who you are, which is "your true self." This may sound very easy, but it is not.

There is a difference between your inner self (self-perception) and your true self. Your true self is the person you are authentically, at your core. It is the part of you that is not influenced by external factors, such as your upbringing, your culture, or the people you surround yourself with.

The goal of correcting self-identity is for your inner self to be aligned with your true self. This means that you believe in who you are authentically, and you live a life that is true to yourself.

Let me explain a little bit here before we proceed, your inner self represents the subconscious image that you hold within yourself. This image is shaped by a myriad of external influences and personal experiences. This subconscious image develops early in life, influenced by familial dynamics, cultural norms, societal expectations, and significant life events. It serves as the lens through which you perceive yourself and interpret the world around you, influencing your beliefs, attitudes, and behaviors.

On the other hand, your true self embodies your purest essence, untainted by external influences, societal expectations, or cultural conditioning. It represents the unadulterated core of your being, where authenticity reigns supreme and your inner wisdom flourishes.

Unlike the inner self, which may be shaped by external pressures and distorted perceptions, your true self transcends these limitations to reveal the unfiltered truth of who you are. At its core, your true self embodies authenticity—a deep alignment with your genuine and original thoughts, emotions, and desires.

It is the unmasked version of yourself, free from the need for approval or validation from others. In essence, your true self is the most honest reflection of your innermost values, beliefs, and aspirations, unencumbered by societal norms or expectations.

When your inner self is not aligned with your true self, you experience conflict and dissatisfaction. You feel like you are not living your true purpose or that you are not being authentic.

Your true self is the key to healthy relationships. Relationships reflect your inner being or self-perception; you will have conflict if your inner being is not one with your true self. The conflicts you have in relationships reflect the conflicts you have within you. If you keep falling in love with people who rip you off and go away, ask yourself what was in those people that attracted you or what you have inside that attracts these people.

When you are connected to your true self, you can say no. Yes is only possible when no is known. It is only possible to say yes to an opportunity or a relationship when you know when to say no. We cannot be jacks-of-all-trades.

Your true self is your most authentic and genuine self. It is the person you are at your core, without any filters or pretense. Your true self is where your potential flows from, and it is the incorporation of your unique gifts and talents.

It is your innate capacity to achieve great things, unburdened by external influences or limiting beliefs. In other words, your true self is the best version of yourself. It is the person you are born to be.

You can only live a fulfilling and meaningful life once you connect your self-perception to your true self. Unharmonized true self and perception often lead to a constant search for meaning and a sense of being adrift. This can lead to a sense of emptiness, dissatisfaction, and conflict. When you connect your inner self to your true self, you become more aware of who you are and what you are meant to do in the world.

You start to make choices and pursue goals that are aligned with your deepest values and beliefs. This leads to a more authentic and fulfilling life, one that is full of meaning and purpose.

Furthermore, your true self serves as a compass for navigating your life's journey with integrity and purpose. When you are in touch with your true self, you experience a profound sense of inner peace, fulfillment, and harmony. Your actions and decisions stem from a place of authenticity and alignment with your deepest values, leading to a life that feels meaningful and fulfilling.

Embracing your true self also means honoring your innate worth and inherent dignity as a human being. It involves recognizing and celebrating your unique qualities, even flaws, your talents, and contributions to the world.

By embracing our true selves, we cultivate a deep sense of self-acceptance and self-love, which radiates outward to positively impact our relationships and interactions with others.

Moreover, the true self represents a state of profound freedom—an emancipation from the shackles of societal expectations and cultural conditioning. It allows us to break free from the need to conform or fit into predefined roles, embracing instead the full spectrum of our authentic selves.

In this state of liberation, we are empowered to express ourselves fully and unapologetically, embracing both our strengths and vulnerabilities with courage and grace.

In essence, the true self is the ultimate expression of our humanity—an unbounded reservoir of love, compassion, and wisdom that resides within each of us. By reconnecting with our true selves, we unlock the door to a life of profound authenticity, purpose, and fulfillment, where we are free to be exactly who we are, unapologetically and unabashedly.

HOW TO CONNECT TO YOUR TRUE SELF

Nothing on earth exists by itself; everything you know or see comes from somewhere. The potential and characteristics of anything come from its source. When you are not connected to your source, you malfunction. You are not fulfilling your intended purpose, and over time, you die. For anyone to function correctly and be all they are supposed to be, they must stay attached to their source.

A mobile device is not alive on its own. It needs to be connected to a power source to operate. When it is connected to power, it gains a measure of life. However, as we use it, the battery drains, and the device malfunctions. Eventually, the battery will die, and the device will no longer work.

A Resource has to stay attached to its source for it to live.

Look at plants and fish! When you uproot a plant from the soil, it doesn't die instantly. Due to stored nutrients, it can survive for a short time. Plants live longer when they find ground to stay connected to. Similarly, fish removed from water do not perish immediately; their lives wither away as their connection to their life-giving environment is cut off. This principle applies to humans, too. You must stay attached to your source to fulfill your potential and be all you can be.

It's becoming a little philosophical, right? I know, but please stay with me for a moment; I am taking you somewhere amazing.

WHERE DO YOU TRULY COME FROM?

This is a question of your source, and it is such a fundamental inquiry that every human being who has ever lived on the planet has at least asked themselves. It starts from where humanity originates, to where we come from as a race, nation, and ethnicity, until eventually, an individual asks themselves where they come from as an individual.

To properly answer this question, you need to see yourself as a whole—body, soul, and spirit

IDENTITY

Human beings are indeed composed of both material and immaterial aspects, creating a complex and multifaceted existence.

The material aspect refers to the physical body—the tangible, observable form that comprises bones, muscles, organs, and tissues. This material body provides the structure and vessel through which we interact with the physical world, perceive sensory stimuli, and engage in various activities. In contrast, human beings' immaterial aspect encompasses the intangible elements that contribute to their consciousness, identity, emotions, thoughts, beliefs, and spirituality.

This immaterial dimension transcends the physical realm and includes aspects such as the mind, intellect, emotions, spirit, and soul. While these components cannot be measured or quantified in the same way as the material body, they play a crucial role in shaping our experiences, perceptions, and interactions with the world around us.

The mind, for example, is a fundamental aspect of the immaterial self, serving as the seat of consciousness and cognitive processes such as perception, memory, reasoning, and imagination. It allows us to process information, form beliefs, make decisions, and engage in complex thought patterns. Similarly, emotions are another vital aspect of the immaterial self, encompassing feelings such as joy, sadness, anger, fear, and love, which color our experiences and influence our behavior.

Beyond the mind and emotions, human beings also possess a spiritual dimension that is often regarded as the deepest and most profound aspect of the immaterial self. This spiritual aspect encompasses beliefs, values, morals, ethics, and the search for meaning and purpose in life. It involves a sense of connection to something greater than oneself—whether it be God, universal consciousness, or transcendent reality—and often manifests through religious or philosophical beliefs, practices, rituals, and experiences.

Ultimately, the material and immaterial aspects of human beings are intricately intertwined, shaping our identities, experiences, and perceptions of reality. While the material body provides the physical framework for our existence, it is the immaterial dimensions of consciousness, emotion, and spirituality that imbue our lives with depth, meaning, and significance. Embracing the full spectrum of our material and immaterial selves allows us to cultivate a holistic understanding of what it means to be human and to navigate the complexities of existence with wisdom, compassion, and purpose.

Both modern science and the founders of philosophy and psychology recognize that these are parts of a complete human being. Plato, a respected Greek philosopher and one of the 3 key founding fathers of philosophy and psychology (the others being Aristotle & Socrates), believed that the soul could exist apart from the body and would exist after the body's death. In addition, modern scientists, such as Watson's Human Caring Theory, suggest that a person has three dimensions: mind, body, and soul.

Your body needs to stay connected to the ground. As a human being, your physical aspect, the body (blood, bones, and tissues/muscles), comes from the soil, and first and foremost, you need to be grounded. Life is a cycle; where a particular thing comes from is where it returns after serving its purpose. Humans and animals come from the ground; they are sustained by depending on the ground and return to the ground after they die. The ecological cycle shows that all organisms return to the ground where they came from and become ground again. You cannot stay in the air (as birds) or in the water (as fish) forever; you must remain on the ground. Being grounded is much more than having your feet on the ground; it's also about recharging your body by feeding it.

This is why you need to eat food from the ground, or at least animals from the ground, to live. When you stop eating, your physical being (body) dies. Nutritionists encourage us to eat natural food grown in the soil and avoid artificial or manufactured food as much as possible because of this principle of being attached to our source.

Your soul needs to stay connected to your family or nation. Your soul is what makes you a social being. (A soul is made up of the mind, emotions, and will.) You come from humans, your parents, and your ancestors. This calls for a longing for emotional belonging. You have an emotional attachment to your roots and historical background. This is where the concept of a motherland and a mother tongue comes from.

To understand how crucial emotional attachment to your source is, consider these two examples: In 1959, Rwanda, our small landlocked country in East Africa, forced many of its people into exile. Some grew to become prominent in exile states. For example, the late Major General Fred Rwigema, of Rwandan origin, was among Uganda's top 5 chief national leaders after capturing Kampala in 1986. The current president of Rwanda, H.E. Paul Kagame, was the deputy chief of military intelligence. So many other soldiers of Rwandan origin were prominent in Uganda, too.

Despite their privileged positions, these top leaders were willing to give up everything they had to fight for a better future for their people. They were willing to sacrifice their comfort and security to liberate their home country; they could not be satisfied elsewhere except back home.

Similarly, when Theodor Herzl, the founder of political Zionism, was offered the chance to begin the state of Israel in East Africa, he said, "We shall build our state and call it Palestine. We shall build it in the place where our fathers lived, where they built and created, and where they gave the world its greatest moral treasures." Why choose a desert in Palestine instead of arable land in East Africa?

Herzl believed that the Jews needed a homeland, and he argued that Palestine was the best choice because of its *historical and emotional significance to the Jewish people*. His argument was not about the wealth of the land; the most important thing was the motherland, the relationship with the source of the Jews, and the land of Palestine.

In our mother tongue, Kinyarwanda, there is a saying, "*Agahugu gataye umuco wako karacika* (a nation that loses its essence or culture stops to exist)." or "*Amazi arashyuha ariko ntiyibagirwa iwabo wa mbeho*" (as much as water may be hot, it will eventually come back to its coldness). In other words, no matter how high you go in life, you will always need to come home to your source, to find your roots, and to be grounded.

Consider these 2 case studies.

Most scholars agree that when the West took the enslaved people out of Africa, one crucial thing they did was break them entirely from their homeland. Physically, they took them out of their ancestral lands. Emotionally, they had to break any emotional ties to their motherland. They did this by forcing them to gradually give up their native languages by forbidding them to use them and teaching them the language of their captors. They changed their names from their native ones to those their masters chose to give them.

They forced them to learn new art, music, and all other things that connected them to their native background.

The story of the ancient father of Israelites, Abraham, was studied as a psychology case study. God tells Abraham to leave his country, kindred, and father's household to the land that He would show him. He literally was told to leave his physical country but also his kindred. The word translated as kindred is the Hebrew word "moledeth" which means your nativity or native land. This was to disconnect himself from his emotional attachment to his motherland, where he was born and grew up.

Your spirit needs to remain connected to its source. Your third aspect of life, which is immaterial and the most critical, is your spirit (conscience, instinct, and supernatural connection).

Where does your spirit come from? You need to figure out clearly where that part of your being comes from and ensure you are correctly connected to it to maximize your potential. Otherwise, while you may not die immediately when disconnected from your Source, you begin to malfunction and diminish, your spiritual vitality gradually decreases, and you eventually die.

So let's develop more on these different concepts for us to understand our true selves so we can shape our authentic and right identity.

I will start with the aspect of our being many have not explored yet, that is your:

YOUR IMMATERIAL SELF

As human beings, we consist of both material and immaterial aspects—a physical body and an intangible soul and spirit. While our physical form derives from the earth, our immaterial essence holds a higher significance in the hierarchy of our being. Let's delve deeper into the immaterial aspects of human existence, beginning with the soul:

THE SOUL:

The soul encompasses the faculties of the mind, emotions, and willpower. The mind processes information, assigning meaning to symbols and synthesizing perceptual inputs to form concepts.

Emotions, on the other hand, are complex psychological states that elicit physiological and cognitive responses, ranging from happiness to sadness, anger, or fear. Willpower embodies the ability to control one's thoughts, exercise self-control, and make decisions in alignment with personal values and beliefs. While the soul is an immaterial aspect of our being, it is relatively easier to comprehend compared to the parts of the spirit: conscience, instinct, and supernatural connection, also known as fellowship.

It's crucial to recognize the significance of our immaterial aspect, as it holds greater importance than our physical form. Our soul is intricately connected to our ancestral roots and cultural heritage, as explored in previous discussions.

IDENTITY

Now, let's turn our focus to the spirit, which we have reserved for further exploration in this chapter.

Understanding the dynamics of the human spirit is essential before delving into how the body, soul, and spirit interact in our daily lives, whether consciously or unconsciously.

SPIRIT:

Your spirit is made up of your conscience, instincts, and supernatural connection. Extended research and science have defined each part. Three main branches of science study the human spirit. That is psychology (the study of mental processes and behavior, including emotions, thinking, and consciousness), philosophy (the study of the fundamental nature of reality, knowledge, and existence), and metaphysics.

Metaphysical studies generally seek to explain inherent or universal elements of reality that are not easily discovered or experienced in your everyday life. As such, it is concerned with explaining the features of reality that exist beyond the physical world and our immediate senses.

Let's first establish how science defines each of these 3 parts of the spirit, and we will then discuss what they have to do with the principles of building healthy relationships.

Conscience is a cognitive-emotional process involving the internal evaluation of one's actions and motivations based on one's moral values and beliefs. This process can lead to feelings of guilt or shame when one has acted in a way that is inconsistent with one's conscience or to feelings of pride or satisfaction when one has acted in a way that is consistent with one's conscience.

You might feel guilty when you do something wrong or feel satisfied when you do something good. Your conscience can also help you make difficult decisions, such as whether or not to stand up for what you believe in, even when it is unpopular.

We often know that something is right or wrong without necessarily rationalizing it, and that is why we say that your spirit is an immaterial aspect that we can't explain.

Instinct, or intuition, is what a person knows they should do based on their innate knowledge and experience. This type of intuition guides a person's actions without conscious thought. Instincts are natural triggers—impulses that drive actions beyond someone's thoughts..

On a metaphysical level, intuition is a direct connection to a higher source of knowledge. It is a method of knowing that is unrestricted by our senses or our logical mind. Metaphysical thinkers have argued that intuition is a way of tapping into the universal mind or the divine. They believe that intuition can provide us with insights into the nature of reality that are beyond the reach of our rational mind.

Fellowship or connection to the supernatural is defined as a transcendent connection that unites all beings. It is a recognition of our shared humanity and interconnectedness with all creation. Metaphysical thinkers have argued that fellowship is not simply a social bond but a spiritual one. They believe that we are all part of a larger whole and that our true nature is one of love and unity.

IDENTITY

This fellowship aspect is where the function of vision resides because, indeed, *vision is the function of the spirit mind; it's not just a product of the intellectual mind.* Vision goes beyond what can be seen with the physical eyes; it is the ability to perceive and understand the deeper truths. It allows us to see beyond the surface level and tap into our innate intuition.

This visionary function allows you to know your place in the grand scheme of things. By tapping into your vision, you can gain clarity on your unique role and purpose in the world. This understanding allows you to make choices and take actions that align with your true self, ultimately leading to a more fulfilling and meaningful life.

It's this supernatural connection through which you can discern the right time to do certain things. You can always sense whether this is the right time to make this move. The right timing is discerned through a deep sense of intuition and awareness. This ability to discern the right timing enhances your decision-making skills and increases the likelihood of success in achieving your goals.

You can also connect with some people in this fellowship/supernatural connection. You will have some seemingly supernatural connection with people. You meet a person, and you connect with them before even talking. Talking to the person convinces the mind, but the connection that happens before talking to someone happens on the supernatural connection level or fellowship function. Such a connection is also based on your instinct.

In Kinyarwanda, we have a saying, "amaraso arakururana," meaning that blood attracts. Throughout history, in different parts of the world, children have connected to their mothers only by feeling some kind of connection, without knowing that they are their mothers. Eventually, they find out that they are related.

You will often meet a person, and as much as their actions and behaviors towards you are fine, somehow you feel inside that you need to avoid this person. That is the function of your spirit; you need to listen. So many people ignore that voice and end up losing their lives or parts of their lives in one way or another.

Your spirit works in ways you may not always understand; more often, it seems out of your control. For example, you might do something, convincing yourself that it is right, but your conscience continues to haunt you. In this case, you are not in full control. Your intuition is not entirely up to you either; you will need to do what it says or not, but it will only sometimes depend on you to do what it says.

THE SOURCE OF YOUR SPIRIT

We defined that your material part comes from the soil (ground), while your soul comes from your ancestry (family ancestry, land of ancestry, etc.) We should have explained the spirit or talked about where it came from. Now that you understand what makes up your spirit, tracking where it comes from is essential.

There are some principles on which we base our understanding of the source of each part:

The first principle of tracking your source discussed previously was that "in the end, everything returns to where it comes from."

The example was that your body, just like that of animals, goes back to the soil/ground after you die.

We also explained that "the law of resemblance (looking alike) tells the source." This kind of resemblance manifests in forms of attribute, functionality, and potential.

For example, Kenyans are known for long-distance running, which flows from generation to generation, while Carribeans are known for speed; they monopolize short-distance running.

You look like the parents from whom you were born; most of the time, you take their personality traits and share some abilities; this is purely genetic rather than socially constructed.

So, where does your spirit come from? Where does it go when life is over? And what does it look like? Who does it resemble?

There are mainly two theories that are believed by the whole world. One is the creation theory; the other is the evolution theory, or what others call Darwinism.

Many scientists with tendencies toward atheism have welcomed the theory of evolution, which suggests the existence of humans through the process of natural selection. Natural selection is the differential survival and reproduction of individuals with favorable traits. Over time, natural selection could lead to the emergence of new species, they said.

Darwinism explains that in the case of humans, *your ancestors were primates (Baboons, Apes, Chimpanzees, and Gorillas) who lived in Africa millions of years ago.* Over time, these primates evolved to become more upright, have larger brains, and develop more complex language and social skills.

However, this theory was disapproved by advanced metaphysical studies that were not as advanced at the time, and more importantly, this theory was debunked by the very person who brought it forward. Darwin wrote a letter to his friend William Graham, saying, "I have never been an atheist in the sense of denying the existence of a God. I think agnosticism would probably be a more correct description of my state of mind."

In fact, it is a theory that many prominent scientists disagree with. Most of them believed in the creation of the universe. Those worthy of mention are:

Galileo Galilei (1564–1642) was an Italian astronomer, physicist, and engineer from Pisa, sometimes described as a polymath. Galileo has been called the "father of observational astronomy", the "father of modern physics", the "father of the scientific method", and the "father of modern science". He is well-known for saying that *"God's hand has written the laws of nature in the language of mathematics."* He also said, *"I give infinite thanks to God, who has been pleased to make me the first observer of marvelous things."* As the chief observer of space, he was so amazed by what he saw that he could only see the creator.

Robert Boyle (1627–1691) was an Anglo-Irish natural philosopher, alchemist, chemist, physicist, and inventor. He is regarded as one of the founders of modern chemistry and is best known for Boyle's law, which describes the inversely proportional relationship between the absolute pressure and volume of a gas.

IDENTITY

Robert Boyle famously said, *"God would not have made the universe as it is unless He intended us to understand it."* He added, *"God [is] the author of the universe and the free establisher of the laws of motion."* He clearly debunks the evolution theory that the world might have come to existence by some accidental forces that brought it forth.

Isaac Newton (1643-1727) was an English physicist and mathematician who is widely recognized as one of the most influential scientists of all time and a key figure in the scientific revolution. His book Philosophiæ Naturalis Principia Mathematica ("Mathematical Principles of Natural Philosophy"), first published in 1687, laid the foundations of classical mechanics.)

Mr. Newton, thinking about the planet, said, *"This most beautiful system of the sun, planets, and comets could only proceed from the counsel and dominion of an intelligent and powerful Being.*

Newton also noted about God that "from true lordship, it follows that the true God is living, intelligent, and powerful; from the other perfections, that he is supreme, or supremely perfect. He is eternal and infinite, omnipotent and omniscient; that is, he endures from eternity to eternity, and he is present from infinity to infinity; he rules all things and knows all things that happen or can happen."

Albert Einstein (1879-1955) was a theoretical physicist who developed the theory of relativity, one of the two pillars of modern physics (alongside quantum mechanics). He received the 1921 Nobel Prize in Physics "for his services to theoretical physics and especially for discovering the law of the photoelectric effect."

Albert is famous for his quote, "God does not play dice," which explains how it is impossible to create a formula in physics laws unless they were intelligently designed. This debunks the theory of evolution that anything could have happened by accident.

He also said that *"science without religion is lame; religion without science is blind."* He explained his personal beliefs: "*My religion consists of a humble admiration of the illimitable superior spirit who reveals himself in the slight details we are able to perceive with our frail and feeble mind."*

When studying the origin of the spirit, the most prominent literature consulted is the Judeo-Christian literature, the Bible, about the creation of the universe. This is only in terms of literature, though, because the creation narrative is embedded in every culture and the core of humanity.

This narrative dates back to human history. Empires and civilizations rose and fell while this narrative persisted. Contrary to what some people say, it is basically not just a Judeo-Christian theory; it is a theory that was believed worldwide, even in cultures that had not interacted with Judeo-Christian literature.

For example, in Rwanda, one of the names we gave to our "God" was "Rurema," meaning Creator. This was long before colonization and any interactions with the Bible. Rwanda is just in East Central Africa.

If you go as far as India, they had a Brahma before interacting with Judeo-Christian literature. Brahma is commonly referred to as the creator god in Hinduism, responsible for creating the universe and all living beings.

IDENTITY

If you jump as far as America, the native Americans believed in Wakan Tanka before interacting with Judeo-Christian literature. Akan Tanka is the Lakota Sioux word for the Great Spirit. It is a term used to refer to the sacred or the divine. Wakan Tanka is often translated as "Great Spirit," but it can also be translated as "Great Mystery." The Lakota people believe that Wakan Tanka is beyond human understanding. Wakan Tanka is the creator of all things. The Lakota believe that Wakan Tanka is present in all things, both animate and inanimate. Wakan Tanka is also the source of all power and knowledge.

Therefore, the theory is not an exclusive belief in Judeo-Christian literature but seems ingrained in humanity. However, Judeo-Christian literature, mainly for Jews, Muslims, and Christians, has extensively explained who this Creator is.

Recently, H.E. Paul Kagame, president of the Republic of Rwanda, explained something that should make sense to everybody. He said, *"The way the universe is designed leads you to ask yourself that all these objects hanging in the air that do not collide, even when they collide, nothing much is damaged; these things are revolving around each other, rotating all the time. You get to a point where you think that there is definitely a power behind it. Even though we may not understand properly what that power is, honestly, we have faith in God, but we believe in God in an unfathomable way, and I think that is what makes God a real God."*

Your source determines who you are: we cannot even start talking about your identity without talking about your source. As discussed earlier, when asked "Who are you?" many people answer by where they come from. Instead of asking, "Who are you?" others will only ask, "Whose son is that?"

This is because your source determines who you are. The soil determines whether it will produce plants or metal ores. Only the creator of the thing determines what that thing is. The rest of the others are only guessing.

Your source determines your potential: The creator of an invention is the only one who decides what that invention will be used for and what problem it is meant to solve. You can never know your purpose (our next book) without knowing your source. *You cannot know your true self without knowing your source.* You will only keep on guessing.

Vision, a function of the human spirit, connects you to your life's purpose and sense of significance. Your vision is the only thing that can determine your future. You do not know your abilities and limitations until you know your source.

Suppose you are serious about your life and serious about mastering relationships. In that case, if you are serious about living a life of significance, you need to decide where you come from. You must understand your source before attempting to know your true identity or the person you truly are.

So again, where do you come from? Who told you who you are? You can read many books and still not understand who you are. Your society and your experiences might be giving you wrong information; if they didn't create you, they have no idea who you are. You are who you are because of the information you receive. *You don't see yourself as you are; you see yourself as you were told. If the information is wrong, you are wrong about who you are, a tragedy.*

IDENTITY

YOUR BODY, SOUL, AND SPIRIT

Your material being (body) and immaterial being (soul and spirit) make you who you are. You are one person in these 3 parts, so these parts should be integrated for you to be a person of integrity. Let us understand how these 3 parts work together.

<u>Your soul is central to your being.</u>

Your soul is made up of three parts (mind, emotions, and will). It's only the will that controls the rest of the parts. Your mind and emotions/feelings seek to influence your will. But your will can choose to act according to your feelings or your mind. That is why you sometimes do things that may not necessarily make sense, and other times, you decide to do something you don't feel.

The body seeks to influence your emotions/feelings or mind so that your will determines what to do. On the other hand, your spirit also seeks to control your mind or feelings so that your will can decide what to do.

Your brain is what connects you to your soul. Your brain is the part that connects every part of your body to your soul. Your brain connects blood, tissue, and bones to your soul. This makes your brain a super-natural computer that is complex to understand. Your brain is responsible for everything that happens to your body; it decides whether the heart should pump or not and all the voluntary and involuntary processes in your body.

For example, your body senses (seeing, hearing, tasting, smelling, and touching) send information through a process called the nervous system to your brain, seeking to stimulate your brain to respond. Your brain has access to both your conscious mind (where you reason before you respond) and your subconscious mind (the auto-response of your mind). Your brain will also bring back information from your mind to every part of your body to do what it is commanded to do.

For example, when you see a snake, your eyes send information to your brain that there is an object in front of you; the eyes send an image to your brain; your brain sends it to your mind; your mind will check in the memory and interpret that this is a snake and it is dangerous; you are advised to run. Your brain receives information again and tells your legs to turn and run. This is the simplest way to explain how it works without using complicated biological terms.

This is how your body will always seek to influence your soul. Your body constantly tells your soul what to feel or think, and your soul can listen or reject.

Your spirit is entirely connected to your soul: Your conscience directly influences your feelings/emotions or mind by talking to you as if it were independent. Your conscience might stimulate thoughts about what you are considering doing by telling you that it is wrong or right; by doing so, it is trying to influence your mind to reach your will and get it to do what is right. After you have done something wrong, your conscience will make you feel guilty; it influences the emotion to reach your will and get it to make remedies.

Your instinct or intuition will also try to influence your emotions/feelings to get your will to act, as will your spirit. Your spirit consistently tries to influence your soul by sending information to your mind and emotions to get your will to do what your spirit wants.

Listen to your spirit more than your body:

Sometimes, your body and spirit will agree to instruct your soul; at that time, you are very lucky. But more often than normal, your spirit and your body may disagree, and it is up to your soul to decide who to listen to.

In that case, listen to your spirit because it knows things beyond what the eyes can see; it connects to your future. If you listen to your conscience, you won't regret it. Your instincts will often protect you from a lot of harmful things. For example, if a person offers to give you a ride during the rain, your body says it's raining; protect me; enter the car; your instincts tell you, I don't feel safe to go with this person. If you don't listen to your instincts, you might end up being kidnapped.

YOUR INTEGRATED SELF IDENTITY

The word "integrity" means being integrated together. Having an integrated self-identity is the goal of life. It is being able to connect your inner being to your true being/self. Your inner self is your belief system; it's what you believe to be true about yourself now, as told by the sources you have interacted with. If the sources know you for sure and your belief system matches who you truly are, then you are integrated. Integrity is a concept deeply rooted in the idea of being whole and fully aligned with oneself. Integrity signifies the state of being integrated, where all the facets of your being come together in perfect harmony. This integration is the ultimate goal of life—a lifelong journey toward becoming one's true and authentic self.

Connect your inner being to your true being.

Your inner being, as already discussed, is your self-perception, your belief system, or simply what you believe to be true about yourself. Your true self, on the other hand, is who you truly are—the person you originally are.

You need to understand your body and its source; this will guide you on how to connect truly to your source and feed your body accordingly. This is the same for your soul; you need to know where you come from and what your ancestors believed. Know as much as you can about your nation and your people, and feed your soul accordingly to stay attached to your source.

More importantly, identify your spiritual source, connect to it, and stay connected to it because only then can you know your true self, your uniqueness, and your purpose.

Your material aspect connects you to physical reality, meaning that your body and senses allow you to interact with the physical world around you. Your soul connects you to your surroundings in an immaterial way, meaning that you are also connected to the world on a deeper level.

Physical space or time are not constraints on this connection. To connect to your future, you need to use your spirituality. This aspect is connected to your soul and to the higher realms of consciousness. When you are able to tap into your spiritual aspect, you can receive guidance and insights about your future.

Only your spiritual source will tell you who your true self is, your reason for existing, your abilities, and your uniqueness. Once you are

IDENTITY

able to reconnect to your spiritual source, everything that makes you who you are will be known to you. This is why it is important to connect to your spirit as soon as possible. Until you connect to your spiritual source, you are not living but simply existing.

If the information you received about yourself was from other sources besides your spiritual source, you don't know who you truly are, and your self-perception is wrong. You do not have integrity because you are not harmonized. In fact, it means that your values and beliefs are wrong, and you destroy more than you build.

You cannot treat people beyond how you treat yourself. If you value your life, you won't take other people's lives. To the extent that you are taking other people's lives, your internal value system must have been messed up to the extent that you don't know who you are. Assassins are prevented from having any personal relationships; they say, these relationships create a weakness in them. Once their life's identity is distorted, once they don't care about their own lives, they won't care about other people's lives.

For your own good, you need to know your identity by reconnecting to your true sources. Only true sources of information can give you original information about you; others are only guessing.

The immaterial identity should be given higher priority than the material identity.

Your body is very important because it allows you to operate on earth; without the body, you are no longer allowed on earth. That is why you need to feed your body with a balanced diet, drink water, exercise, and literally take care of your body for you to operate here.

However, when it comes to identity, your material aspect should submit to your immaterial aspect.

The dangers of placing your material (physical being) higher than your immaterial are very devastating. If you put your material being higher than your immaterial being, you will be very limited to the physical realm. You will not be able to interact, for example, with people who are different from you.

The greatest tragedy of our generation, the 94 genocide against the Tutsi, which claimed the lives of over a million people in just 100 days, stemmed from a grievous distortion of perception.

It reduced individuals to mere physical entities, stripping away their inherent humanity and perpetuating a profoundly distorted view of existence. This reductionist perspective, divorced from the rich tapestry of human experience and interconnectedness, paved the way for unspeakable atrocities to unfold unchecked.

At the heart of this tragedy lay a dehumanizing ideology that vilified an entire Tutsi group, casting them as lesser beings devoid of intrinsic worth or dignity. Such toxic beliefs, propagated through propaganda and prejudice, fostered an environment where compassion gave way to cruelty, and empathy yielded to enmity.

In the eyes of the perpetrators, their victims were reduced to mere objects, stripped of their humanity and relegated to the status of disposable entities. This distorted perception not only fueled the machinery of genocide but also corroded the moral fabric of our society, blinding individuals to the inherent sanctity of human life.

By reducing others to mere physical beings, devoid of agency or autonomy, perpetrators absolved themselves of accountability and justified unspeakable acts of violence. The consequences of this distorted view reverberate to this day, leaving scars that may never fully heal and lessons that must never be forgotten.

In confronting the legacy of such atrocities, we are compelled to reaffirm the fundamental humanity of every individual and reject the dehumanizing ideologies that seek to divide us. Only by recognizing and honoring the inherent dignity of every human being, regardless of ethnicity, religion, or background, can we hope to transcend the cycle of violence and build a future grounded in compassion, understanding, and respect.

Central to this reevaluation is the recognition of humans not merely as physical beings but as imbued with an immaterial essence—a soul and spirit. This acknowledgment expands our understanding of humanity beyond the confines of the material world, embracing the profound interconnectedness that binds us all. By embracing this holistic view of human existence, we reaffirm the intrinsic value of every individual and confront the pernicious ideologies that seek to diminish our shared humanity.

However, in Rwanda, the distortion extended even beyond the realm of perception, penetrating deeply into the physical aspect of human existence.

In Rwanda, during pre-colonial times, there were basically 3 socio-economic classes. The first classes are Tutsi (the top class), the Hutu (the middle class), and Twa (the lower class).

In all the known history of Rwanda, there had never been any conflict between these 3 groups of the same nation or people; they had freely intermarried, and some would move from being one group or category to another. That was until another source of information about Rwanda's identity came in from European colonizers, who said they had made many studies about races and such. They tried to make these groups into tribes or ethnicities.

Political scientists know the term "big" lie"—the idea that if a false statement or narrative is repeated frequently and emphatically enough, it can become widely accepted or believed, even when there is no factual basis for it. Rwandans were deceived way too much to start believing that they were indeed different ethnicities or tribes.

The truth is that Rwandans do not have tribes or ethnicities. By definition, a tribe is a social group that shares a common ancestry, language, culture, and territory. Tribes are often characterized by their strong sense of community and shared identity. Ethnicity is a social construct that refers to a shared cultural identity based on common ancestry, language, religion, customs, and traditions.

If this is the case, Rwandans are of the same tribe or ethnicity because they share common ancestry, language, culture, territory, customs, and traditions. Wrong sources of information (colonizers) provided wrong information about the identity of Rwandans, and it resulted in genocide.

The so-called differences between Hutu, Tutsi, and Twa are so completely fabricated that even testing the DNA of the three groups proved that even physical or biological differences are non-existent.

IDENTITY

One study, published in the journal Nature in 2004, analyzed the DNA of over 1,000 people from Rwanda, including Hutu, Tutsi, and Twa. The study found that the three groups were genetically very similar, with only minor differences in the frequency of certain genetic markers (which is even common for biological brothers).

Another study, published in the journal PLOS ONE in 2012, analyzed the DNA of over 4,000 people from Rwanda and Burundi, including Hutu, Tutsi, and Twa. The study found that there was no significant genetic difference between the three groups, even when controlling for factors such as geography and socioeconomic status.

If the 94 genocide against Tutsi, which claimed over a million lives, was simply a fabrication that was not based on anything tangible whatsoever, does that not show you that your self-perception of who you are is not only detrimental to society but also to your own life?

Human life is infinite.

Your identity is not confined solely to your origins; it encompasses the entirety of your existence, including your present circumstances and your aspirations for the future.

The human capacity for imagination expands the scope of life beyond the confines of temporal boundaries, infusing each moment with the potential for growth and transformation. Indeed, to define oneself solely by the past is to limit the vast expanse of possibilities that lie ahead.

Central to understanding one's identity is recognizing the pivotal role of the spirit in shaping the trajectory of one's life. The spirit serves as a compass, guiding individuals toward their future endeavors and aspirations. Without a clear sense of direction, one risks stagnation, trapped in a state of inertia where personal growth remains elusive.

As the Rwandan proverb wisely suggests, *"utamenya iyo iva ntamenya iyo ajya,"* "he who does not know where he comes from cannot know where he is going." This timeless wisdom underscores the interconnectedness of past, present, and future in shaping one's sense of self.

The aftermath of trauma casts a long shadow, leaving profound scars on the spirit, soul, and body of survivors. For those who endured the horrors of the 94 genocide against the Tutsi, the impact is immeasurable, resonating through every aspect of our being.

At the core of our existence lies a fractured spirit, shattered by betrayal and devastation. Many sought solace within the sanctuary of churches only to be met with betrayal. Many found their trust in institutions shattered, along with their faith in humanity itself.

Yet, amidst the ruins of our shattered spirit lies the resilience to rise from the ashes and reclaim our sense of purpose and identity.

The relentless injustice and absence of accountability inflicted a deep wound upon our conscience, leaving behind a sense of moral injury. Yet, within the depths of our wounded souls, lies the capacity for forgiveness and reconciliation, paving the way for healing and redemption.

IDENTITY

The survivor's connection to their homeland was severed, and that is a wound on the soul. The nation that should have protected them became their persecutor. This betrayal shattered their sense of belonging, a feeling further eroded by years of propaganda denying their Rwandan identity. The rupture of the connection to homeland represents a profound wound, severing the ties that bind many to their roots. Yet, within the depths of the wounded souls, lies the resilience to reclaim our sense of belonging and cultural identity, forging a path towards rebuilding our national unity.

The deliberate targeting of Tutsis based solely on identity strikes at the very essence of who a human being is, instilling a profound sense of fear and insecurity.

Yet, within the depths of these wounded souls, lies the courage to confront the past, embrace the true identity, and build a better future.

As we navigate the path to healing and restoration, we must remember that healing is a journey, not a destination. It requires courage to confront the darkness of the past, patience to allow time for healing in the present, and hope to envision a brighter future.

In embracing your true identity, you reclaim your power and agency, transforming your pain into purpose and your scars into strength.

Together, we forge a path towards healing, reconciliation, and a future filled with hope and possibility.

While acknowledging the importance of one's origins, it is equally crucial to embrace the dynamic nature of identity, which extends beyond mere historical context. Your past serves as a foundation upon which to build, but it does not dictate the entirety of your being.

You are a multifaceted individual, continuously evolving and unfolding through the interplay of past experiences, present circumstances, and future aspirations.

Embracing this holistic perspective allows you to cultivate a deeper understanding of who you are and who you strive to become.

In conclusion, this chapter reveals that identity is not a static entity but rather a dynamic construct shaped by a myriad of interconnected factors. Your material being, encompassing biological elements like genetics and brain chemistry, lays the groundwork for temperament and physical traits, yet it's merely a piece of the puzzle.

Your family and social environments wield significant influence. They provide the context within which values, traditions, and cultural norms are absorbed, thereby shaping your sense of self within society.

Cultural and societal influences further mold your identity, with norms, expectations, and trends acting as guiding forces in self-perception and interaction with others.

Your personal experiences and relationships, from triumphs to setbacks and from intimate bonds to fleeting connections, contribute richly to the tapestry of identity, instilling values, beliefs, and a sense of belonging.

IDENTITY

Moreover, self-reflection and introspection serve as pivotal tools in the ongoing journey of self-discovery, allowing individuals to refine their understanding of themselves amidst life's complexities.

This journey is not linear but punctuated by developmental stages and life transitions, each offering opportunities for introspection and growth. In essence, identity formation is a multifaceted odyssey, woven from the threads of biology, upbringing, culture, personal experiences, and introspection.

It is not a destination but a continual process of exploration and redefinition, echoing the sentiment that identity is as much about becoming as it is about being.

I want to close this chapter by reminding you that: Your future is not merely a distant destination waiting to be reached; rather, it is the guiding force that shapes the trajectory of your past. When you embark on a journey of self-discovery, delving into the depths of your spirit to uncover your purpose and reason for existence, you realize that the narrative of your life unfolds in reverse. It is through connecting with your innermost being that you gain clarity on the interplay between past, present, and future. Each moment becomes imbued with significance as you recognize the intricate dance of causality that weaves the fabric of your identity.

Your past experiences, whether characterized by triumph or tribulation, serve as stepping stones leading toward the realization of your future potential. In this paradigm, your identity transcends the confines of linear time, encompassing the entirety of your existence in a seamless continuum.

At the heart of cultivating a true sense of identity lies the imperative of seeking information from the most authentic source—the spiritual realm. In a world inundated with misinformation and distortion, your spiritual identity serves as a beacon of truth, illuminating the path toward self-realization and empowerment.

Unlike external labels or societal constructs, which impose limitations and constraints, your spiritual essence transcends all boundaries, offering boundless freedom and possibility.

By grounding yourself in your spiritual identity, you liberate yourself from the shackles of conventional norms and expectations, embracing a life of authenticity and purpose.

It is through this profound connection to your spiritual source that you unlock the latent potential within, propelling you toward the realization of your highest aspirations. In the realm of the spirit, there are no barriers, no limitations—only the infinite expanse of possibility stretching out before you, waiting to be explored.

In a nutshell, "Relating to yourself" isn't just about superficial self-care or fleeting moments of self-indulgence. It's about forging a profound and authentic relationship with the deepest layers of your being. This entails delving into the depths of your soul, confronting your fears, insecurities, and vulnerabilities, and embracing every facet of your identity with unwavering acceptance and love.

When you relate to your true self, you embark on a journey of self-discovery and self-acceptance that transcends societal norms or external validations. It's about recognizing and honoring your innate worth, regardless of how others perceive you or what expectations they may impose upon you.

This journey requires courage, vulnerability, and a willingness to confront the parts of yourself that you may have long ignored or suppressed. Being connected to your true self empowers you with a profound sense of self-awareness and understanding.

It's about peeling back the layers of conditioning, societal expectations, and past experiences to uncover the essence of who you truly are. This level of introspection allows you to discern your authentic desires, values, and aspirations, guiding you toward a life that aligns with your deepest truths.

Moreover, relating to your true self equips you with the clarity and resilience needed to navigate life's challenges with grace and purpose. By embracing your strengths and weaknesses alike, you cultivate a sense of inner balance and harmony that transcends external circumstances. This inner alignment empowers you to make decisions from a place of authenticity and integrity rather than succumbing to external pressures or societal norms.

In essence, relating to yourself is a sacred journey of self-discovery, acceptance, and empowerment. It's about honoring your unique essence, embracing your imperfections, and embracing the full spectrum of your humanity with unwavering compassion and love. As you embark on this transformative journey, may you find solace in the depth of your own being and emerge more fully aligned with your true self.

As we draw the curtains on this chapter, let's reflect on the essential insights and lessons we've uncovered:

Embrace Authenticity: The journey of self-discovery and acceptance begins with embracing your authentic self. Allow yourself to be vulnerable, acknowledging both your strengths and weaknesses without judgment or self-criticism.

Cultivate Self-Awareness: Develop a deep sense of self-awareness by exploring your emotions, beliefs, values, and aspirations. This self-awareness serves as a compass, guiding you towards decisions and actions that align with your true essence.

Practice Self-Compassion: Be kind and compassionate towards yourself, especially during moments of difficulty or self-doubt. Treat yourself with the same level of empathy and understanding that you would extend to a dear friend.

Honor Your Needs: Recognize and honor your needs, whether they be physical, emotional, or spiritual. Prioritize self-care and self-nurturing activities that replenish your energy and nourish your soul.

Challenge Limiting Beliefs: Identify and challenge any limiting beliefs or negative self-talk that may be holding you back. Replace these with empowering affirmations and beliefs that affirm your worth and potential.

Celebrate Your Uniqueness: Celebrate the uniqueness of your journey and the beauty of your individuality. Embrace your quirks, passions, and idiosyncrasies as essential components of what makes you authentically you.

Seek Growth and Expansion: Remain open to growth and expansion, welcoming new experiences, perspectives, and opportunities for self-discovery. Embrace the inherent fluidity and evolution of the self, knowing that growth often occurs outside your comfort zone.

Nurture Self-Connection: Cultivate a daily practice of self-reflection, mindfulness, or meditation to deepen your connection with your inner self. Create sacred moments of stillness and solitude where you can listen to the whispers of your soul.

Forge Meaningful Connections: Surround yourself with supportive and nurturing relationships that honor and uplift your true essence.

Seek out communities and connections where you can authentically express yourself without fear of judgment or rejection.

Trust the Journey: Trust in the process of self-discovery and acceptance, knowing that it is a lifelong journey filled with twists, turns, and unexpected revelations. Embrace each moment as an opportunity for growth and self-realization.

As you carry these key takeaways forward, may they serve as guiding lights on your path toward greater self-discovery, acceptance, and fulfillment. Remember, the journey of self-discovery is not about reaching a destination but rather about embracing the beauty and complexity of the journey itself.

CHAPTER 3
HEALING THE
FAMILY BONDS

Rebuilding the foundation of family relationships after the trauma of genocide. Creating a safe and nurturing environment for familial support and connection.

The trauma of genocide leaves indelible scars not only on individuals but also on the very fabric of society. In the case of the 94 genocide against the Tutsi in Rwanda, the devastation wrought by this tragedy reverberates across generations, profoundly affecting families and communities.

The first target of the genocide was the family unit itself, as it sought to not only exterminate individuals but also to obliterate the bonds that held families together. As a result, the genocide left around 100,000 children orphaned, disrupting the very foundation of familial relationships and leaving lasting wounds that continue to shape the lives of survivors.

Family is the cornerstone of our social fabric, serving as the nucleus of our community and the bedrock of our identity. Within the familial unit, individuals find connection, belonging, and support, shaping their understanding of themselves and the world around them.

Whether bound by blood, marriage, adoption, or a sense of shared responsibility and care, family ties run deep, providing a sense of continuity and belonging across generations.

The concept of family extends beyond mere biological relationships to encompass a broader network of kinship and affinity. From nuclear families comprising parents and children to extended families encompassing grandparents, aunts, uncles, and cousins, the familial unit takes on diverse forms reflective of cultural, social, and historical contexts. Each family structure brings its own dynamics, traditions, and values, contributing to the rich tapestry of human experience. At its core, the family serves as the first and most influential social group individuals encounter, shaping their early experiences, beliefs, and behaviors.

From the moment of birth, family members play a pivotal role in nurturing, educating, and socializing individuals, instilling in them fundamental values, manners, and worldviews. It is within the familial embrace that individuals learn the importance of love, respect, cooperation, and resilience, laying the groundwork for their interactions with the wider world.

Moreover, the family unit serves as a microcosm of society, reflecting its dynamics, challenges, and opportunities. Within the family, individuals learn to navigate interpersonal relationships, resolve conflicts, and negotiate shared responsibilities, skills that prove invaluable in their interactions with others beyond the familial sphere. By fostering a sense of solidarity, empathy, and mutual support, families cultivate the essential social bonds that underpin cohesive and resilient communities.

FAMILY

In the aftermath of trauma, such as the genocide against the Tutsi in Rwanda, the family unit becomes even more crucial as a source of solace, healing, and resilience. Despite the profound disruptions and losses inflicted by genocide, families retain their capacity to nurture hope, rebuild relationships, and forge a path forward. By drawing upon the strength of familial bonds, survivors can find comfort in shared experiences, support one another through grief and trauma, and envision a future rooted in resilience and renewal. As survivors endeavor to rebuild the foundation of family relationships after the trauma of genocide, they must recognize the pivotal role of family in their healing journey.

By fostering open communication, empathy, and forgiveness, families can transcend the wounds of the past and forge deeper connections built on trust, understanding, and mutual respect. Through collective healing and reconciliation, families can reclaim their sense of identity, belonging, and purpose, laying the groundwork for a brighter and more hopeful future for generations to come.

A family is meant to be a sanctuary, a place where love flows freely and acceptance is unconditional. It's a haven where one can shed all pretenses and be embraced for exactly who they are, flaws and all.

For many Rwandans, however, this idealized notion of family remains elusive, shattered by the brutalities of genocide that left countless children orphaned and bereft of the nurturing bonds of familial love. Growing up without the guiding presence of a loving family can leave deep scars on the psyche, shaping one's understanding of self and relationships in profound ways.

Without the anchor of familial acceptance, individuals may internalize a sense of inadequacy, believing that they must conform to certain expectations to be worthy of love and belonging. The absence of a nurturing family environment can have far-reaching consequences, extending into the very fabric of future relationships and interpersonal dynamics. Without the foundational experiences of safety, acceptance, and love within the family unit, individuals may struggle to form healthy connections with others, perpetuating a cycle of relational challenges and emotional disconnection.

The blueprint for relationships is often laid within the family, where individuals learn the intricacies of communication, trust, and intimacy. For those who have been deprived of this foundational groundwork, navigating the complexities of interpersonal relationships can feel like an insurmountable task.

Despite the profound wounds inflicted by the genocide, many survivors have endeavored to build their own families, seeking to create a sense of belonging and continuity amidst the chaos and loss. However, the unhealed traumas of the past continue to cast a long shadow over these new familial bonds, influencing dynamics and interactions in subtle yet significant ways.

The legacy of trauma can manifest in various forms, from difficulties in expressing emotions to challenges in establishing boundaries and fostering intimacy. In their quest for acceptance and love, some may resort to maladaptive coping mechanisms, such as substance abuse or risky behaviors, further exacerbating the cycle of trauma and dysfunction.

At the heart of these struggles lies a profound sense of insecurity and unworthiness, born from the ruptured foundation of self-acceptance and belonging. Without the anchoring presence of familial love and acceptance, individuals may grapple with feelings of isolation and alienation, seeking validation and approval from external sources. The quest for acceptance becomes a desperate pursuit, driving individuals to compromise their well-being and integrity in search of fleeting moments of connection.

In order to break free from the shackles of intergenerational trauma and forge healthier, more resilient familial relationships, it is imperative to confront the wounds of the past with courage and compassion. By acknowledging the impact of trauma on both individual and collective psyches, survivors can begin the journey of healing and reconciliation, laying the groundwork for a future rooted in resilience and renewal. Through the transformative power of self-awareness, empathy, and forgiveness, individuals can reclaim their sense of agency and self-worth, paving the way for deeper connections and meaningful relationships grounded in authenticity and acceptance.

The trauma of sexual assault during genocide represents an egregious violation of one's most intimate boundaries, leaving indelible emotional wounds that reverberate through the fabric of individual and familial life.

For survivors of the 94 genocide against the Tutsi in Rwanda, where an estimated 100,000 to 250,000 women were subjected to rape, the aftermath of such atrocities casts a long shadow over their lives and the lives of their families. Rape during wartime is often wielded as a weapon of terror, systematically employed to instill fear, shatter familial bonds, and decimate communities.

In the case of the 94 Genocide against the Tutsi, the pervasive use of sexual violence was not only aimed at inflicting physical harm but also at altering the ethnic composition of future generations, perpetuating a cycle of trauma and suffering that spans generations. The psychological toll of sexual assault, compounded by the specter of HIV/AIDS and the complexities of raising children born from such violence, creates a profound and enduring challenge for survivors and their families.

The scars of trauma run deep, infiltrating every aspect of daily life and eroding the foundations of trust, security, and intimacy within familial relationships. For mothers who bear the burden of caring for children conceived through rape, the challenges are particularly acute, as they navigate the complexities of parenting while grappling with their own unresolved trauma and the stigma associated with their children's origins. Rebuilding family bonds in the wake of such trauma is a daunting task, fraught with emotional landmines and logistical hurdles.

How does one begin to forge connections in the aftermath of unspeakable violence and loss? How can trust be rebuilt when betrayal and abandonment have been etched into the fabric of one's existence? These are the questions that haunt survivors as they strive to reclaim a sense of normalcy and belonging amidst the wreckage of their past.

Yet, amidst the darkness, there exists a glimmer of hope—a resilience that defies the odds and a strength that emerges from the depths of despair. Survivors of sexual violence in conflict are not merely victims; they are agents of change, architects of their own futures.

FAMILY

By confronting their trauma with courage and resilience, survivors can begin the arduous journey of healing, forging new pathways of connection and belonging within their families and communities.

The process of rebuilding family bonds begins with acknowledging the pain and suffering that has been endured, honoring the resilience that has sustained them through the darkest of times. It requires creating safe spaces for survivors to share their stories, to be heard and validated without judgment or stigma. It entails fostering a culture of empathy and support, where survivors and their families can lean on each other for strength and solace.

Ultimately, rebuilding family bonds after the trauma of sexual violence requires a collective commitment to healing and reconciliation. It demands a recognition of the interconnectedness of all humanity, a shared responsibility to bear witness to the suffering of others and to stand in solidarity with those who have been marginalized and oppressed. In the face of unspeakable horror, it is the bonds of family and community that offer a glimmer of hope, a beacon of light guiding survivors on their journey toward healing and wholeness.

Healing from trauma is a multifaceted journey that begins with the courageous act of acceptance—acknowledging the painful realities of the past while embracing the possibility of a brighter future.

To embark on this path of healing is to confront the wounds of the past with compassion and resilience, refusing to be defined by the traumas that have shaped one's life. It requires a willingness to bear witness to the pain and suffering that have been endured, to sit with the discomfort of vulnerability and uncertainty, and to cultivate a sense of self-compassion and self-worth in the face of adversity.

Healing is not a linear process; it is messy, nonlinear, and often fraught with setbacks and challenges. Yet, it is also a journey of profound transformation and growth, a testament to the resilience of the human spirit. Choosing to heal means making a conscious decision to reclaim agency over one's life, to no longer be held captive by the past but to chart a course toward a future filled with hope and possibility.

It is about recognizing that while the wounds of the past may never fully heal, they do not have to define who you are or dictate the trajectory of your life. Instead, healing is about embracing the inherent power within oneself to shape one's own destiny and to rewrite the narrative of one's life in a way that is empowering and liberating. Central to the process of healing is the cultivation of self-awareness and self-compassion—learning to listen to the inner voice that whispers of resilience and strength, even in the darkest of moments. It is about extending grace and forgiveness to oneself, acknowledging that healing is not about erasing the scars of the past but about learning to live with them in a way that is empowering and life-affirming. It is about recognizing that true healing comes from within, from the depths of one's own heart and soul, and cannot be found in external validation or approval.

Moreover, healing from trauma is a journey that is best undertaken with the support of others—whether it be friends, family, or professional therapists. It is about building a network of support and connection, creating safe spaces where one can share their stories and be heard without judgment or shame. It is about finding strength in the community, drawing upon the collective wisdom and resilience of those who have walked a similar path.

FAMILY

In essence, healing from trauma is a deeply personal and transformative journey that requires courage, resilience, and self-compassion. It is about acknowledging the pain of the past while choosing to embrace the possibility of a future filled with hope, healing, and possibility. Above all, it is about recognizing the inherent worth and dignity within oneself, reclaiming agency over one's own life, and stepping boldly into the light of a new day.

There is another challenge for many families: the intermarriage between Hutus and Tutsis. This was once a testament to the unity and cohesion within Rwandan society. However, the atrocities of the 94 genocide against the Tutsi shattered this once vibrant social fabric, leaving behind a fractured and deeply wounded nation. For those born into these intermarried families, the genocide presented a unique and deeply complex challenge—how to navigate their identity in a society torn apart by violence and division.

Raised in households where the lines between Hutu and Tutsi were blurred, these individuals found themselves caught in the crossfire of ethnic hatred and violence. They were neither fully Hutu nor fully Tutsi, but rather occupied a liminal space between these two identities. In a society where ethnic identity was a matter of life and death, this ambiguity left many feeling lost and adrift, struggling to reconcile their sense of self with the harsh realities of their surroundings. The genocide not only robbed these individuals of their loved ones but also of their sense of belonging and identity. With families torn apart and communities decimated, the bonds that once held Rwandan society together were irrevocably severed.

In the aftermath of this unspeakable violence, many found themselves adrift in a sea of uncertainty, grappling with questions of identity, belonging, and purpose.

Attempts to reconcile these conflicting identities often proved futile, as the wounds of the past continued to fester and bleed into the present. For some, the trauma of the genocide became an insurmountable barrier, preventing them from fully embracing either their Hutu or Tutsi heritage. Others found themselves ostracized and marginalized by society, deemed traitors or outsiders for daring to straddle the divide between ethnic groups.

The destruction of the social fabric of Rwanda was not only a loss for those directly impacted by the genocide but for society as a whole. The interwoven tapestry of Hutu, Tutsi, and Twa cultures that once defined Rwandan identity was torn apart, leaving behind a fragmented and fractured nation. In the absence of trust, empathy, and understanding, suspicion and resentment took root, further exacerbating the divisions that had torn the country apart.

Yet, even in the midst of such profound loss and devastation, there remains hope for reconciliation and healing. As Rwanda continues to rebuild in the aftermath of the 94 genocide against the Tutsi, there is an opportunity to forge a new sense of national identity—one that transcends ethnic divisions and embraces the richness and diversity of Rwandan society. By acknowledging the pain and trauma of the past and working together to build a more inclusive and equitable future, Rwanda can begin to stitch back together the torn social fabric of its nation and move forward as a united and resilient society.

Today, as Rwandans strive to rebuild our nation from the ashes of the past, there is a growing recognition that true healing and reconciliation can only come through unity and solidarity. No longer defined by ethnic divisions and labels, we are all Rwandans, bound together by a shared history and a common destiny.

The national unity that we seek today is not merely a lofty ideal but a practical necessity—a way to harness the same forces that once tore us apart and transform them into building blocks for a more just, equitable, and inclusive society.

In this new Rwanda, the divisions that once fueled violence and hatred are being replaced by bridges of understanding and empathy. We are learning to see past the superficial differences that once divided us and focus instead on the bonds that unite us as a people. Whether Hutu, Tutsi, or Twa, we are all part of the rich tapestry of Rwandan society, each contributing our own unique perspectives, talents, and experiences to the collective fabric of our nation.

At the heart of this new vision for Rwanda is a commitment to embracing our shared heritage, language, and culture. No longer defined by the arbitrary distinctions of ethnicity, we are reclaiming our identity as Rwandans, proud of our history and hopeful for our future.

We recognize that we did not choose our parents or the circumstances of our birth, but we can choose how we respond to the challenges and opportunities that life presents us. By focusing on what unites us rather than what divides us, we can begin to heal the wounds of the past and forge a path toward a brighter tomorrow.

It is a journey that will require courage, compassion, and a willingness to confront the painful truths of our history. But it is also a journey filled with hope and possibility, as we work together to build a society that is more just, more inclusive, and more resilient than ever before. As we look to the future, let us remember the lessons of the past and draw strength from the resilience and determination of the Rwandan people.

Together, we can overcome the challenges that lie ahead and build a nation that is truly worthy of the sacrifices made by those who came before us. In doing so, we honor the memory of those we lost in the 94 genocide against the Tutsi and ensure that their legacy lives on in the vibrant, united, and inclusive Rwanda of tomorrow.

IMPORTANCE OF A FAMILY UNIT AND HOW TO REBUILD IT TODAY

The family unit serves as the cornerstone for understanding and navigating relationships throughout one's life. Within the family, individuals learn fundamental skills such as communication, emotional expression, conflict resolution, and empathy. These early lessons provide the framework for how individuals interact with others outside the family circle.

For example, witnessing healthy communication and conflict resolution within the family can foster similar behaviors in future relationships, promoting understanding and cooperation. Conversely, experiencing negative patterns within the family dynamic may lead to challenges in forming healthy relationships later in life.

Families play a pivotal role in shaping an individual's identity, values, and beliefs. During childhood and adolescence, family members serve as primary sources of information and influence. From basic manners to cultural traditions, religious beliefs, and ethical principles, much of what individuals learn about the world stems from their family environment. These shared values and beliefs form the basis of familial identity and contribute to a sense of belonging and cohesion within the family unit.

Moreover, the transmission of cultural heritage and traditions from one generation to the next fosters a sense of continuity and connection to one's roots, enriching the family experience and strengthening bonds between family members.

Perhaps one of the most critical functions of the family is providing emotional support and fostering a sense of belonging. In times of crisis or adversity, family members often rally together to offer comfort, guidance, and assistance. Whether coping with illness, loss, or personal setbacks, having a supportive family network can significantly impact an individual's emotional well-being and resilience. Knowing that there are loved ones who care deeply about one's happiness and success can instill a sense of security and confidence, enabling individuals to navigate life's challenges with greater resilience and optimism.

As we delve into families' significance, it's imperative to acknowledge their profound impact not only on individuals but also on the broader fabric of society. Indeed, understanding the role families play in national building is essential for comprehending the intricate dynamics of social development and progress.

Nations are built on families because families serve as the primary transmitters of culture, values, and societal norms. The beliefs and behaviors instilled within families influence the collective identity and character of a nation.

Addressing the information consumed within families is essential to altering the social fabric of a nation. When families are strong and thriving, they impart essential values such as morality, patriotism, and a sense of community to their children. These values, rooted in familial teachings, form the foundation upon which society operates.

The preamble of the Constitution of the Republic of Rwanda highlights the central role of families in upholding national values. It emphasizes the importance of family, morality, and patriotism in shaping the nation's identity. Strong families contribute to the development of responsible and compassionate citizens who are committed to the common good. By instilling these values within the family unit, nations cultivate a sense of unity and cohesion among their citizens, fostering social harmony and stability.

Research and surveys in the United States of America (USA) consistently demonstrate the impact of stable families on societal success. Studies have shown that adolescents who report strong family bonds are more likely to thrive in various aspects of life. These adolescents exhibit higher levels of well-being, academic achievement, and emotional resilience compared to their peers from less stable family environments.

Family connection provides children with a safe and nurturing environment to explore their identities, develop their strengths, and navigate life's challenges. Family stability is crucial for individual well-being and national security. Numerous statistics in the USA underscore the correlation between stable families and lower rates of crime, delinquency, and violence.

For instance, research has found that a significant percentage of individuals involved in US school shootings grew up in unstable family environments. Similarly, children from fatherless homes are more likely to engage in criminal activities and experience incarceration. The presence of a stable family structure, particularly with engaged fathers, significantly reduces the likelihood of juvenile delinquency and incarceration.

Moreover, family stability has broader implications for societal security. Teachers and law enforcement officials identify the lack of parental supervision at home as a significant factor contributing to violence in schools. Policymakers can enhance national security and mitigate various social challenges by promoting family stability and strengthening parental relationships.

Stable families serve as a protective buffer against youth violence and crime, contributing to safer communities and a more resilient society. Therefore, supporting initiatives that prioritize family stability is essential for fostering a secure and prosperous nation.

Despite the challenges posed by the destruction of the traditional family structure during the genocide against the Tutsi in Rwanda, it is essential to recognize the enduring significance of family bonds. While many individuals may have grown up without the traditional nuclear family, it is crucial to acknowledge the importance of family in providing love, support, and a sense of belonging.

However, rebuilding families may require unconventional approaches, such as embracing the notion of a chosen family or adoption. By redefining the concept of family to include individuals who share common goals, values, and aspirations, survivors of genocide can create new familial bonds based on love, trust, and mutual respect.

Embracing Adoption and Chosen Family: Adoption represents one avenue through which individuals can build families based on choice rather than biological relations. However, the concept of adoption extends beyond the traditional understanding of bringing non-biological children into the family.

It encompasses the broader principle of intentionally choosing to form familial bonds with individuals who share common values, goals, and aspirations. In this sense, adoption becomes a symbol of resilience and renewal as survivors of genocide embrace the opportunity to create new family structures that transcend biological ties. By embracing the notion of a chosen family, survivors can forge meaningful connections with others who provide love, support, and a sense of belonging, thereby rebuilding the social fabric of their nation and fostering a future characterized by unity, compassion, and resilience.

The impetus behind my decision to write this book stems from a profound desire to illuminate the many challenges confronting individuals in the aftermath of trauma while concurrently offering a beacon of hope—a roadmap toward surmounting these seemingly insurmountable obstacles.

When I confront the daunting task of rebuilding family bonds in the wake of the unimaginable tragedy of the 94 genocide against the Tutsi, it can feel like an insurmountable feat, especially when viewed through the lens of social science analysis. Yet, in the depths of despair, I find solace and inspiration in the indomitable spirit of the Rwandan people—a spirit akin to resilient seeds lying dormant in the soil, awaiting the nurturing touch of providence to usher forth their vibrant growth. Just as seeds buried beneath the earth emerge from their slumber, breaking through the hardened crust to bask in the warm embrace of sunlight, so too do we possess an innate capacity for renewal and regeneration.

FAMILY

The metaphorical burial inflicted upon us by the atrocities of history did not extinguish our essence; rather, it served as the catalyst for our rebirth—a testament to the unwavering resilience that courses through our veins. Like seeds scattered upon fallow ground, we were buried, but we were seeds—seeds that refused to succumb to the darkness, seeds that germinated and took root, defiantly sprouting forth with renewed vigor and vitality.

Thus, as we navigate the arduous terrain of healing and reconciliation, let us draw strength from the latent potential within us, knowing that just as seeds unfurl their tender shoots in defiance of adversity, so too shall we emerge from the ashes of despair, resolute in our commitment to cultivate a future imbued with hope, unity, and prosperity.

Reflecting on the example of the Netherlands, a nation renowned for its innovative approach to living below sea level, offers valuable insights into the power of leveraging disadvantages as opportunities for growth. Despite facing significant challenges due to its low-lying geography, the Netherlands has transformed adversity into advantage through strategic water management and engineering solutions. By embracing their unique circumstances and investing in forward-thinking infrastructure and technologies, the Dutch have not only mitigated the risks associated with living below sea level but also positioned themselves as global leaders in resilience and sustainability.

Living below sea level presents numerous challenges and disadvantages, including the constant threat of flooding, land subsidence, soil salinization, high infrastructure costs, environmental impact, and vulnerability to climate change.

However, rather than viewing these obstacles as insurmountable barriers, the Netherlands has approached them as opportunities for innovation and adaptation. Through a combination of strategic planning, technological advancements, and proactive policies, the Dutch have successfully navigated the complexities of their environment while simultaneously thriving in various domains.

The Netherlands' journey towards harnessing its geographical disadvantage began with a fundamental shift in perspective—from viewing vulnerability as a limitation to recognizing it as a catalyst for innovation and progress. This paradigm shift paved the way for the development of innovative solutions and sustainable practices that not only addressed immediate challenges but also fostered long-term resilience and prosperity.

Drawing parallels between the challenges faced by Rwandan genocide survivors and the innovative spirit of the Netherlands, it becomes evident that adversity can serve as a catalyst for positive change when approached with determination and ingenuity.

By acknowledging our disadvantages and embracing them as opportunities for growth and transformation, we can chart a new course for rebuilding family bonds and fostering social cohesion. Through collective resilience, unity, and a shared commitment to overcoming adversity, we can emerge stronger, united, and thriving, demonstrating to the world that even in the face of unimaginable tragedy, hope and renewal are possible. As we embark on this journey of healing and reconciliation, let us take solace in the knowledge that every achievement begins with a single step, and together, we can pave the way for a brighter future for generations to come.

CHAPTER 4

NAVIGATING SPOUSAL RELATIONSHIPS

The preceding chapter delved into families' pivotal role in shaping individuals and their influence on community and national development. However, to truly understand family dynamics, we must focus on their fundamental cornerstone: marriage.

Indeed, marriage is the bedrock upon which families are built, providing the framework for nurturing relationships and fostering a sense of stability and belonging.

In this chapter, we will explore the significance of marriage in family dynamics, its impact on societal cohesion, and the essential principles for cultivating solid and resilient marital relationships. Additionally, we will address the profound impact of events such as the 94 genocide against the Tutsi on marriages, examining the challenges they pose and strategies for overcoming them. By exploring these themes, we aim to shed light on the complexities of marriage in the context of societal upheaval and to offer insights into building successful and thriving marriages as a cornerstone of stable families and a cohesive nation.

Marriage is the foundation and backbone of any family, exerting a profound influence on the well-being of its members and the broader society. When marriages falter, families inevitably suffer, leading to dysfunctionality that permeates various aspects of life. The impact of marital discord extends beyond the couple to affect their children academically, socially, and emotionally.

Studies have shown that children from unstable families are more prone to engage in self-detrimental behaviors, such as alcohol consumption and drug abuse, in the absence of parental guidance and supervision. The lack of a stable family structure can exacerbate societal issues, contributing to higher rates of crime, substance abuse, and mental health problems.

Recognizing the pivotal role of marriage in shaping family dynamics and societal well-being, it becomes imperative to invest in strengthening marital relationships from the outset. Research underscores the importance of parental relationship quality in influencing children's behavior, academic performance, and emotional well-being. Stable and loving marriages provide children with a nurturing environment for their development, fostering resilience and positive social outcomes.

Moreover, the significance of marriage extends beyond the family unit to impact individuals' professional lives and overall societal productivity. Employees' personal lives can significantly affect their job performance, highlighting the need for workplaces to accommodate employees' challenges and provide supportive resources. Additionally, statistics reveal that children of divorced parents are more likely to experience health problems, academic difficulties, and behavioral issues, underscoring the profound implications of marital instability on future generations.

MARRIAGE

Furthermore, the absence of a father figure in children's lives has been linked to adverse outcomes, including higher rates of high school dropout, behavioral problems, and infant mortality. Fathers play a crucial role in supporting their children's education and overall well-being, emphasizing the importance of paternal involvement in family life.

Conversely, divorce or separation can have detrimental effects on spouses' physical and mental health, increasing the risk of mortality from various causes.

The centrality of marriage in fostering family stability and societal well-being cannot be overstated. By prioritizing the maintenance and restoration of marital relationships, we can mitigate the adverse consequences of marital discord on individuals, families, and communities. Through targeted interventions and support systems, we can empower couples to cultivate healthy, resilient marriages as the cornerstone of thriving families and vibrant societies.

By its very nature, marriage is a complex and intricate union—a merging of two individual lives, each on their unique journey through the labyrinth of existence. It entails navigating the intricacies of human relationships, with all their joys, challenges, and uncertainties.

Yet, when we consider the profound impact of devastating events such as the 94 genocide against the Tutsi in Rwanda, the complexity of marriage is magnified exponentially. The trauma and scars left by such atrocities linger in the hearts and minds of survivors, shaping their perceptions, behaviors, and relationships in profound ways.

In the context of marriage, this trauma adds a layer of complexity as many grapple with the weight of their past experiences while striving to forge a shared future with their partner. The aftermath of genocide leaves an indelible mark on the collective psyche of a nation, infiltrating even the most intimate aspects of people's lives. Therefore, examining the intersection of marriage and trauma from such catastrophic events offers invaluable insights into the resilience, challenges, and dynamics of marital relationships in the face of adversity.

The strain of the 94 genocide against the Tutsi on the spousal relationships in Rwanda left indelible scars on the fabric of society. Historical divisions between individuals from Tutsi and Hutu backgrounds created deep-seated barriers that impeded the possibility of intermarriage, even among those who found themselves deeply in love. Despite genuine affection, the lingering trauma of the past erected insurmountable walls between communities, preventing them from forging marital bonds based on mutual understanding and acceptance.

The wounds of the genocide ran so deep that they overshadowed the potential for love to transcend historical grievances, leaving many couples torn apart by the weight of their shared history.

The urgency to establish a family in the aftermath of the genocide often eclipsed the readiness for marriage among survivors. The profound desire for stability and a sense of belonging drove many individuals to hastily enter into marital unions without fully comprehending the magnitude of their commitment. In their eagerness to rebuild what was lost, they overlooked the complexities and challenges of building a successful and enduring marriage.

Consequently, marriages founded on such shaky ground were vulnerable to instability and dissolution as the partners grappled with the realities of their new lives together. The psychological aftermath of the genocide cast a long shadow over the decision to marry for many survivors.

Deep-seated feelings of self-hatred, survivor's guilt, and existential despair plagued individuals who questioned their very right to exist in a world stained by unspeakable atrocities. In the absence of a clear sense of purpose or identity, entering into marriage became a risky endeavor, fraught with uncertainty and insecurity. Marrying without a firm foundation of self-awareness and emotional resilience left many survivors vulnerable to the tumultuous winds of marital discord and disillusionment.

Moreover, the socio-political landscape of post-genocide Rwanda was fraught with complexities that hindered genuine connections between individuals. Lingering historical grievances and pervasive mistrust between communities created an atmosphere of suspicion and apprehension, making it challenging for survivors to form authentic relationships based on mutual respect and love. The scars of the past loomed large, casting doubt on the possibility of finding happiness and fulfillment in the arms of another. In such a climate of uncertainty and distrust, the prospect of entering into marriage seemed daunting, if not impossible, for many survivors.

Many survivors experienced profound loss, not only of their loved ones but also of the sense of security and belonging that comes from having a family; for those who found themselves displaced or without proper care, adoptive families often provided inadequate support and failed to meet their emotional needs. In such circumstances, marriage became a tempting escape route—a means of establishing transactional arrangements and a sense of stability and belonging. However, viewing marriage as a mere escape from hardship rather than a lifelong commitment built on love and mutual respect sets the stage for inevitable disappointment and disillusionment.

Marriage should never be entered into as a way to flee from one's problems or to fill a void left by past traumas; rather, it should be a conscious and intentional decision made with a clear understanding of its profound implications. Moreover, the profound loss experienced by many survivors of the genocide left them emotionally numb and disconnected from the joys and aspirations of married life.

The absence of their own families robbed them of the excitement and anticipation that typically accompanies the prospect of marriage. In Rwandan culture, marriage is a union between two individuals and a celebration of family and community. Without a supportive network of family members to share in their joy and excitement, many survivors found themselves lacking the emotional investment and enthusiasm necessary to embark on the journey of marriage. The absence of familial ties diminished the significance of marriage in their eyes, leaving them feeling adrift and disconnected from the cultural traditions and values that once held meaning for them.

Faced with such daunting obstacles, many individuals settled for marriages of convenience, seeking companionship or security rather than genuine love and partnership. This pragmatic approach to marriage, driven by a desire for stability and social acceptance, often resulted in unions devoid of passion or emotional connection. Instead of serving as a source of joy and fulfillment, these marriages became mere transactional arrangements, perpetuating a cycle of dissatisfaction and unhappiness for all involved.

MARRIAGE

In essence, the legacy of the genocide casts a long shadow over the institution of marriage, making it difficult for individuals to form meaningful and fulfilling partnerships based on love, trust, and mutual respect.

But as we talk about all of these, if you find yourself grappling with the sense that your marriage and family have been adrift due to the multitude of challenges stemming from the traumatic events of the 94 genocide, it's essential to understand that there is hope for reconciliation and renewal. As we embark on this journey together, I want to assure you that you don't have to remain mired in despair or resignation. Instead, we will explore strategies and insights to help you navigate the complexities of rebuilding your marriage and restoring harmony to your family life.

To illustrate this process, let's consider the analogy of a train that has veered off its tracks or a bicycle with a slipped chain. In both scenarios, you can not go anywhere before you fix the problem. The first step toward rectifying the situation is to identify where things went wrong and take proactive steps to correct the course. Similarly, in your marriage, it's crucial to examine the underlying issues and challenges that have contributed to its breakdown. By acknowledging these areas of discord and addressing them head-on, you can begin the process of rebuilding your relationship on a stronger and more solid foundation. Recreating your marriage requires a willingness to confront uncomfortable truths and make necessary changes. It's not about assigning blame or dwelling on past mistakes but rather gaining clarity on what went wrong and charting a path toward healing and renewal. Just as a broken bicycle chain must be repaired before you can resume your journey, so too, you must address the fractures in your marriage before you can move forward together as a couple.

To fix your marriage, it's essential to have a clear understanding of what constitutes a healthy and fulfilling marital relationship. This involves learning about effective communication, conflict resolution, and emotional intimacy. By gaining insight into these key areas, you can develop the skills and tools needed to navigate the challenges of married life and cultivate a relationship built on mutual respect, trust, and love.

Furthermore, it's important to approach the process of rebuilding your marriage with compassion and empathy for yourself and your spouse. Recognize that both of you are human beings with strengths and weaknesses and that mistakes are a natural part of the journey. Rather than dwelling on past failures or shortcomings, focus on how you can learn and grow from them together. By fostering a spirit of forgiveness and understanding, you can create a supportive and nurturing environment for your relationship to thrive.

Seeking professional guidance and support can also be instrumental in the process of rebuilding your marriage. Marriage counseling, therapy, and support groups can provide valuable insights and tools for overcoming obstacles and strengthening your bond as a couple. A qualified therapist and/or a relationship coach can help you explore underlying issues, improve communication skills, and develop strategies for resolving conflicts effectively. Don't hesitate to reach out for help if you feel overwhelmed or stuck in your efforts to repair your marriage.

In conclusion, while the challenges posed by the legacy of the 94 genocide against the Tutsi may seem daunting, it's important to remember that there is always hope for healing and reconciliation. By acknowledging the areas where your marriage went wrong, committing to making necessary changes, and seeking support when needed, you can rebuild your relationship and create a future filled with love, trust, and happiness.

In all you will read in the next few pages, keep in mind that through this journey of healing and rebuilding, three essential stages will emerge: awareness, acceptance, and action.

Awareness is the initial step towards transformation. It involves recognizing and understanding the areas where your marriage has been impacted by traumatic events in the past. By becoming aware of the patterns, behaviors, and dynamics that have contributed to the challenges in your relationship, you can gain clarity on the areas that require attention and intervention.

Secondly, **acceptance** is crucial in the process of healing. It entails acknowledging the reality of your situation, including the pain, struggles, and mistakes that have shaped your marriage. Acceptance does not mean resigning yourself to a fate of unhappiness but rather embracing the truth of your circumstances with compassion and self-compassion. It involves letting go of blame, resentment, and unrealistic expectations and, instead, embracing the imperfections and complexities of your relationship with humility and grace.

Finally, **action** is the key to transformation and renewal. It involves taking deliberate and intentional steps towards positive change in your marriage. Once you've become aware of the challenges in your marriage and have accepted them as part of your reality, the next step is to take action to address them and initiate positive change. This involves actively implementing strategies, making decisions, and engaging in behaviors that support your healing journey.

During the action phase, you may find yourself exploring various therapeutic modalities, seeking support from friends or professionals, and implementing coping mechanisms to manage the challenges effectively. This may include seeking professional help, engaging in couples therapy, counseling, or coaching, practicing effective communication skills, setting healthy boundaries, and prioritizing self-care and mutual support. Action also involves facing difficult emotions and situations head-on rather than avoiding or suppressing them. It requires courage, resilience, and a willingness to confront discomfort in pursuit of growth and healing.

By taking intentional steps towards healing, you empower yourself to reclaim agency over your life and relationships and work towards a more positive and fulfilling future. In essence, the action phase is about translating awareness and acceptance into tangible progress and positive change. It's about actively engaging in the healing process and taking proactive steps to cultivate resilience, well-being, and personal growth. By embracing this phase wholeheartedly, you set yourself on a path toward greater empowerment and renewal of relationships, leading to fulfillment and wholeness.

Ultimately, the key to a successful marriage lies in practicing open communication, fostering emotional intimacy, prioritizing mutual respect and understanding, and cultivating a spirit of forgiveness and empathy. By embracing these principles and committing to them wholeheartedly, you can lay the groundwork for a fulfilling and enduring partnership that stands the test of time. Remember, it's never too late to turn your marriage around and embark on a journey of renewal and growth together.

HOW DO YOU BUILD AND SUSTAIN A SOLID MARRIAGE?

As we transition to our next discussion, we will delve into the best practices for fostering a solid and enduring marriage. By exploring these principles, you'll gain valuable insights into what constitutes a healthy and thriving marital relationship. We'll use these insights as a diagnostic tool to assess your current situation and identify areas where adjustments may be needed. It's essential to recognize that while you cannot change the past, you hold the power to shape your present and future. Embracing this responsibility empowers you to take proactive steps toward building the fulfilling and lasting marriage you desire. Let's embark on this journey of self-discovery and transformation together as we uncover the keys to unlocking a lifetime of love and happiness in your marriage.

As we embark on this journey of reclaiming and revitalizing marriages, it's crucial to understand that marriage is akin to crafting an omelet. Just as the quality of an omelet is determined by the ingredients used, the strength and health of your marriage are shaped by the individuals within it. Just imagine: if you were to prepare an omelet and included a rotten egg, the entire dish would be tainted. Similarly, the dynamics of your marriage reflect the essence of both you and your spouse.

Therefore, as we navigate the path toward restoring your marriage, it's essential to recognize that you hold a significant degree of influence over the outcome. While you cannot control every aspect of your spouse's behavior or attitudes, you have full power and responsibility over your own actions, attitudes, and contributions to the relationship. Your choices, attitudes, and behaviors serve as the foundational ingredients that shape the overall quality and vitality of your marriage.

As we delve deeper into the process of revitalizing your marriage, remember that true transformation begins with self-awareness and personal growth. By taking ownership of your role within the relationship and committing to positive change, you can lay the groundwork for a stronger, more fulfilling partnership. So, as we progress on this journey, keep in mind that the journey toward a revitalized marriage starts with you. Embrace this opportunity for self-reflection and growth, and let it guide you toward a brighter future for both yourself and your marriage.

Now, let's embark on a discussion centered around the three fundamental cornerstones of a thriving marriage: trust, transparency, and tolerance. When we refer to these elements as cornerstones, we are likening them to the foundational stones upon which a sturdy structure is built. In the context of marriage, they represent the bedrock upon which a strong and enduring relationship is established. Just as a building's cornerstone anchors the structure and ensures its stability, these principles serve as the starting point for cultivating a successful and fulfilling marital union.

Before delving into the three cornerstones of a successful marriage, it's crucial to recognize the paramount importance of preparation in the marital journey. As Abraham Lincoln famously remarked, "If I had six hours to chop down a tree, I would spend the first four sharpening the axe." This analogy underscores the significance of adequate preparation before embarking on any endeavor, including marriage. Unfortunately, many individuals underestimate the value of preparation, often deferring the learning process until they are already in the throes of marriage. However, research suggests that between 50-75% of divorces could have been avoided with sufficient preparation. Premarital counseling, while beneficial, often occurs too late in the process – after the choice of spouse has already been made.

MARRIAGE

Effective marriage preparation must begin long before selecting a partner, focusing on personal growth and understanding one's own values, beliefs, and aspirations.

Indeed, the adage "an ounce of prevention is worth a pound of cure" holds particularly true in the context of marriage. Insufficient preparation for marriage can lead to significant challenges and difficulties down the road, necessitating considerable effort, time, and emotional investment to rectify. When couples enter into marriage without adequate preparation, they may find themselves grappling with issues related to trust, communication, compatibility, and conflict resolution.

These challenges can erode the foundation of the relationship and lead to feelings of frustration, resentment, and disillusionment. Redeeming the time in such circumstances requires a concerted effort to address underlying issues, heal relational wounds, and rebuild trust and intimacy. This process often involves seeking professional counseling or therapy to gain insight into the dynamics of the relationship and develop effective strategies for resolution. It may also require couples to engage in open and honest communication, confront difficult truths, and make necessary changes to their behavior and attitudes. Redeeming the time in marriage is not an easy task and may entail periods of discomfort, vulnerability, and pain.

It requires couples to confront their shortcomings, acknowledge their mistakes, and commit to personal and relational growth. However, the rewards of investing in the restoration and revitalization of the marriage can be profound, fostering greater intimacy, connection, and fulfillment for both partners.

Ultimately, the key to redeeming the time in marriage lies in a willingness to confront challenges head-on, seek support when needed, and work together as a team to overcome obstacles and build a stronger, more resilient relationship. While the process may be challenging, the opportunity to heal, grow, and deepen the bond between partners is well worth the effort.

As I said earlier, the foundation of a successful marriage rests upon three crucial cornerstones: trust, transparency, and tolerance.

Trust, as the first cornerstone of a successful marriage, serves as the bedrock upon which the entire relationship is built. It encompasses essential elements such as emotional intimacy, mutual respect, and reliability between partners. Far more than a mere expectation, trust represents a deep commitment to honesty, fidelity, and vulnerability within the marital bond. It necessitates a willingness to place one's faith in the integrity and intentions of the other, forging a sense of security and assurance within the relationship. Without trust, a marriage is akin to a house built on shifting sands, lacking the solid foundation necessary for growth, connection, and longevity.

Trust forms the basis of emotional intimacy, allowing partners to open their hearts fully to one another, share their deepest thoughts and feelings, and cultivate a profound sense of closeness and understanding. It also fosters mutual respect, as partners honor each other's boundaries, opinions, and autonomy, creating a sense of partnership and equality in the relationship. Moreover, trust is essential for establishing reliability and dependability within the marital bond. When partners trust one another, they can rely on each other to fulfill their commitments, honor their promises, and support each other through thick and thin.

MARRIAGE

This reliability creates a sense of stability and security within the relationship, enabling partners to weather life's challenges and uncertainties with confidence and resilience.

In essence, trust is the cornerstone upon which all successful marriages are built, providing the essential foundation for emotional connection, mutual respect, and enduring commitment. It requires vulnerability, courage, and a steadfast belief in one's partner's integrity. By prioritizing trust and nurturing it through open communication, honesty, and consistency, couples can create a relationship characterized by intimacy, resilience, and lasting love.

Transparency, as the second cornerstone of a successful marriage, is intricately linked with trust and mutual respect, forming an essential pillar of emotional intimacy and connection within the relationship. It encompasses the quality of being open, honest, and authentic in one's communication and actions with one's partner, creating a space where vulnerability and acceptance can flourish.

In a transparent marriage, partners feel empowered to share their thoughts, feelings, and experiences openly and honestly, without fear of judgment or rejection. This openness fosters a deep sense of intimacy, understanding, and mutual respect as partners learn to communicate openly and authentically with each other. Transparency lays the groundwork for deeper emotional connection and intimacy, as partners feel safe and secure in expressing themselves fully and authentically.

It allows couples to navigate challenges and conflicts with honesty and integrity, fostering a sense of unity and partnership in the face of adversity. Moreover, transparency promotes acceptance and validation within the relationship as partners learn to embrace each other's vulnerabilities and imperfections with compassion and empathy. In a transparent marriage, partners feel accepted and valued for who they are, creating a strong foundation of trust and intimacy that can withstand the test of time.

In essence, transparency is essential for building a strong and healthy marriage. It provides the framework for open communication, emotional connection, and mutual understanding. By prioritizing transparency and nurturing it through honest and authentic communication, couples can create a relationship characterized by trust, intimacy, and lasting fulfillment.

Tolerance, as the third cornerstone of a successful marriage, plays a crucial role in fostering acceptance and understanding within the marital relationship. It complements trust and transparency by encouraging partners to embrace each other's differences, imperfections, and idiosyncrasies with empathy and compassion. Rather than viewing differences as sources of conflict or division, tolerance enables couples to recognize and respect each other's unique perspectives, beliefs, and behaviors, even when they diverge from their own.

In a tolerant marriage, partners approach conflicts and disagreements with grace and respect, seeking to understand each other's viewpoints and find mutually beneficial solutions. Rather than allowing disagreements to escalate into destructive patterns of communication or behavior, couples prioritize empathy, understanding, and compromise, creating a supportive and harmonious dynamic. Tolerance also promotes a sense of unity and partnership within the relationship, as couples learn to appreciate and celebrate each other's differences rather than allowing them to create barriers or divisions.

By embracing tolerance, couples cultivate a deep sense of connection and mutual respect, laying the foundation for a resilient and enduring partnership. In essence, tolerance is essential for building a strong and healthy marriage, providing the framework for navigating challenges and conflicts with empathy, understanding, and grace. By prioritizing tolerance and embracing each other's differences with compassion and respect, couples can create a relationship characterized by trust, intimacy, and lasting fulfillment.

By prioritizing trust, transparency, and tolerance, couples lay the groundwork for a resilient and enduring partnership. These three cornerstones serve as the essential building blocks of a successful marriage, providing the framework for trust, intimacy, and resilience within the relationship. Trust forms the bedrock of emotional connection and reliability between partners. It is cultivated through honesty, fidelity, and vulnerability, creating a solid foundation upon which love and partnership can thrive. Transparency complements trust by fostering open communication and authenticity within the relationship. By sharing thoughts, feelings, and experiences openly and honestly, partners create a space where they feel accepted and valued for who they are. Tolerance, the third cornerstone, promotes acceptance and understanding of differences, allowing couples to navigate conflicts and disagreements with grace and compassion.

By embracing each other's unique perspectives and beliefs, partners foster a sense of unity and partnership within the relationship. Together, these cornerstones provide couples with the tools they need to withstand life's inevitable challenges and weather storms. As we delve deeper into each cornerstone, let us explore how they can be nurtured, strengthened, and integrated into our own marital relationships to cultivate greater harmony, connection, and fulfillment.

If you are not yet married, these cornerstones are going to guide you into building a solid foundation for your marriage. On the other hand, if you are already married and have seen some important stones lacking, it is a good time to identify the Off-Track Moments: Just like a train that has veered off its tracks or a bicycle with a slipped chain, it's crucial to pinpoint the moments where your marriage went off course. Reflect on your relationship journey and identify key events, conflicts, or challenges that contributed to the breakdown of trust and communication. By understanding the root causes of marital discord, you can begin to address them effectively and chart a course for reconciliation and growth.

Once you've identified the areas where your marriage went wrong, you need to be curious and thoughtful about owning your actions and words that have contributed to the problem so you can be in a good position to start repairing the broken links in your relationship. This may involve having difficult conversations with your spouse, acknowledging past mistakes, and taking responsibility for your actions. It's essential to approach this process with humility, empathy, and a willingness to listen and learn from each other. By addressing unresolved issues and conflicts, you can begin to rebuild trust and intimacy in your marriage.

Just as a train needs to be brought back on track and a bicycle chain needs to be fixed before you can move forward, your marriage requires intentional effort and commitment to recreate it in the right way. This involves redefining your shared goals, values, and priorities as a couple and creating a roadmap for the future. Take the time to envision the kind of marriage you want to build together and commit to making it a reality. By recommitting to each other and investing in your relationship, you can overcome past challenges and create a stronger, more resilient partnership.

Learning from Mistakes: Recognize that mistakes are a natural part of any relationship journey and an opportunity for growth and learning. Instead of dwelling on past failures or shortcomings, focus on how you can use them as lessons to inform your future actions. Be open to feedback from your spouse and willing to make necessary adjustments to improve your relationship. By embracing a mindset of continuous improvement and personal growth, you can create a marriage that is built to withstand the tests of time.

Seeking Professional Guidance: Don't hesitate to seek outside help and support if you're struggling to repair your marriage on your own. Marriage counseling, therapy, and support groups can provide valuable insights and tools for overcoming challenges and rebuilding trust and intimacy. A qualified therapist or coach can help you navigate difficult conversations, address underlying issues, and develop effective communication and conflict-resolution skills. Remember that seeking help is a sign of strength, not weakness, and can provide you with the support you need to create a happier, healthier marriage.

By following these steps and committing to the process of rebuilding your marriage, you can overcome the challenges posed by the legacy of the 94 genocide against the Tutsi and create a relationship that is based on love, trust, and mutual respect. With patience, perseverance, and a willingness to learn and grow, you can rebuild your marriage from the ground up and create a brighter future for yourself and your family.

But let me add a practical touch here, If you find that your marriage lacks a solid foundation of trust, transparency, and/or tolerance, there are steps you can take to repair and rebuild your relationship.

The first step is to return to the beginning, reconnecting with the desire and capacity to restore your marriage. Rebuilding a marriage requires a willingness to revisit the foundational elements that brought you together and rediscover the commitment to making your relationship work.

To rebuild trust, start by prioritizing accountability and taking small, consistent steps to demonstrate your reliability and integrity to your partner. This may involve setting clear boundaries, following through on promises, and openly communicating about your actions and intentions. By creating guardrails and honoring your commitments, you can begin to rebuild the trust that may have been eroded over time.

If transparency is lacking in your marriage, focus on cultivating vulnerability and authenticity in your communication with your spouse. Be willing to let your guard down and share your thoughts, feelings, and experiences openly, even if it feels uncomfortable at first. Start small by sharing small insights or moments of vulnerability, gradually building towards deeper levels of trust and intimacy in your relationship.

In addressing issues of tolerance, it's important to cultivate flexibility and adaptability within yourself. Recognize that differences are inevitable in any relationship and be willing to embrace them with an open mind and heart.

Sometimes, this may require letting go of rigid expectations or preconceived notions and embracing a spirit of compromise and collaboration. By finding common ground and working towards mutual understanding, you can foster greater harmony and acceptance within your marriage.

While some issues may require external assistance or professional guidance, many challenges can be addressed through a combination of self-reflection, communication, and mutual effort. By committing to the process of rebuilding your marriage and investing in the foundational principles of trust, transparency, and tolerance, you can create a stronger, more resilient partnership that withstands the tests of time and adversity.

Now that we've explored the cornerstones of marriage, let's delve into the foundation upon which every solid marriage is built—the 3Cs of a successful marriage: Common goal, Commitment, and Communication.

COMMON GOAL

Marriage is a journey you embark on together, and it is impossible to go together if you have not established the destination beforehand. It does not make sense to ask someone to accompany you when you do not know where you are going yourself. It is essential, before even considering marriage, to have a sense of your own purpose and destiny. You need to have given direction to your life so that when you are looking for someone to accompany you on that journey, you know where you are going. As a wise man once said, two people cannot go together if they do not agree on the destination.

The concept of "Common Goal" speaks to the shared vision and purpose that couples need to establish to move forward. This involves identifying shared values, aspirations, and goals for the future of the relationship. By having a clear understanding of what you are working towards together, you can create a sense of unity and direction that guides your efforts to work on, repair, and strengthen your bond.

Common goals provide a framework for aligning individual aspirations with the overall goals of the relationship, ensuring that individual pursuits complement and support the growth of the relationship as a whole. Setting common goals creates a shared vision for your future together, encompassing shared dreams, aspirations, and desires, providing a roadmap for your journey as a couple. When couples work towards common goals, it fosters a sense of unity and shared responsibility, bringing them together in a collaborative effort to strengthen their bond.

It serves as a guiding principle for making important decisions in the relationship, ensuring that choices align with the shared vision and aspirations of the couple. In times of challenges or disagreements, couples with common goals have a foundation for approaching conflict resolution constructively, drawing upon their shared vision and objectives to find mutually agreeable solutions. Having common goals provides motivation and commitment for both partners, fueling their desire to overcome obstacles and achieve shared aspirations. It deepens the emotional connection and intimacy between couples, creating shared experiences and mutual support. Finding common goals requires a willingness to explore each other's interests and passions seeking opportunities for shared activities and pursuits.

It involves compromise and communication to identify areas of mutual interest and create a shared vision for the future.

By focusing on shared goals and aspirations, couples can strengthen their bond and create a foundation for a fulfilling and enduring relationship. As couples evolve and grow together, they learn to incorporate their unique passions and interests into the broader framework of their shared goals, creating a sense of purpose and fulfillment in their journey together.

COMMITMENT

Commitment forms the solid foundation upon which the marriage rests. True commitment goes beyond mere words—it requires unwavering dedication, loyalty, and perseverance, even in the face of challenges and adversity.

This commitment extends first towards the shared goal established by the couple before it is directed towards each other. The reason the goal of marriage must be common is that one does not seek a spouse who is solely committed to them; instead, they seek someone equally committed to the shared objectives. Couples who are deeply committed to their goals and each other prioritize their relationship, making sacrifices and compromises when necessary to ensure its strength and longevity.

The commitment we are talking about here isn't about blind optimism or ignoring the challenges that lie ahead. Instead, it is about acknowledging the difficulties, recognizing the value of their relationship, and making a conscious choice to work through them together. This commitment is what sustains couples through the ups and downs of life together, providing the anchor that keeps them grounded during turbulent times.

Commitment is rooted in a deep belief in the value and potential of marriage. It is the conviction that the relationship is worth fighting for despite the challenges that may arise. Commitment means being willing to engage in open, honest, and respectful communication, even when it is difficult. It involves a willingness to compromise, listen to different perspectives, and work towards mutually agreeable solutions. Commitment requires prioritizing the needs and well-being of the relationship above individual desires or pursuits. It involves making time for each other, nurturing shared interests, and actively seeking ways to strengthen the bond. Moreover, commitment means being willing to forgive past hurts and move forward. It involves letting go of resentment and focusing on the positive aspects of the relationship and the shared future.

Research by the University of Denver on reasons for divorce pointed out that the number one reason for divorce was "lack of commitment," at 70%. Some participants reported that commitment within their relationships gradually eroded until there was not enough commitment to sustain the relationship, while others reported more drastic drops in commitment in response to negative events, such as infidelity. The researchers give two testimonies from their respondents that illustrate this: "I realized it was the lack of commitment on my part because I didn't really feel romantic towards him. I had always felt more like he was a friend to me." "It became insurmountable. It got to a point where it seemed like he was no longer really willing to work [on the relationship]. All of the stresses together and then what seemed to me to be an unwillingness to work through it any longer was the last straw for me."

Commitment is the foundation of a thriving marriage. It is the unwavering dedication that binds couples together, providing the strength and resilience needed to navigate challenges, overcome obstacles, and emerge stronger than ever before.

By embracing commitment, couples can transform the power struggle stage into an opportunity for deeper understanding, renewed love, and a marriage that stands the test of time.

COMMUNICATION

Communication serves as the essential bridge that connects partners, fostering understanding, empathy, and effective collaboration. Despite its crucial role, communication often remains misunderstood and underutilized in marital relationships, leading to misunderstandings, conflicts, and the erosion of marital bonds.

Communication is the cement that holds the marriage together, forming the very foundation upon which the connection is built. Without effective communication, marital bonds would be fragile, leaving spouses feeling disconnected and adrift. Strong communication skills are vital for building and sustaining a healthy marital relationship, enabling couples to navigate challenges and conflicts with grace and understanding.

It involves a reciprocal process of conveying and receiving messages, ensuring that both partners feel heard, valued, and understood. Verbal communication, encompassing spoken, written, and sign language, is the most overt form of communication within marriage. However, nonverbal communication, such as body language, facial expressions, and tone of voice, plays an equally significant role in conveying emotions and intentions.

In the marital context, nonverbal cues often convey nuances of affection, support, or distress, shaping the emotional landscape of the relationship. Yet, despite their importance, they are frequently overlooked in communication, leading to misinterpretations and discord. The research underscores the detrimental impact of ineffective communication in marriages, with misunderstandings and conflicts often stemming from misinterpretations of verbal and nonverbal signals. By honing their communication skills, couples can mitigate the risk of misunderstandings and cultivate deeper emotional connection and intimacy in their marriage.

To improve communication within marriage, couples must prioritize active listening and effective speaking. Active listening involves giving undivided attention to one's partner, understanding their feelings and perspectives, and providing verbal and nonverbal feedback to demonstrate engagement. Effective speaking, on the other hand, entails expressing oneself clearly, honestly, and respectfully, tailoring the message to resonate with the partner's interests and needs. Moreover, couples should be receptive to feedback and open to making adjustments to enhance their communication skills continually. By fostering open, honest, and empathetic communication, couples can strengthen the foundation of their marriage, building a resilient bond that withstands the trials and tribulations of life together.

Effective communication in marriage empowers couples to navigate their differences in a constructive and respectful manner, facilitating the identification of underlying issues and the discovery of mutually beneficial solutions. By fostering open and honest dialogue, couples can cultivate emotional intimacy and connection, providing a platform for sharing their deepest thoughts and feelings with trust and vulnerability.

Moreover, communication serves as a conduit for developing empathy and compassion within the marital dynamic. As partners actively listen to each other's perspectives and validate their experiences and emotions, they foster a deeper understanding of one another, strengthening their bond of mutual respect and support. The significance of communication in marriage cannot be overstated, as research indicates that it is a leading contributor to divorce rates, accounting for a substantial 65%. This underscores the critical importance of investing in proper and effective communication strategies to mitigate the risk of marital discord and dissolution.

To communicate effectively, couples must recognize that both the content and delivery of their messages are equally vital. Many couples mistakenly assume they are effectively communicating, only to realize later that their approach is flawed.

Furthermore, it's essential to acknowledge that men and women often have distinct communication styles and needs within marriage. Statistics reveal intriguing insights into the communication dynamics between genders. For instance, a significant portion of men identify nagging or complaining as a top irritant in marriage, followed closely by a perceived lack of appreciation from their spouses. Conversely, women commonly express frustration with their partners talking excessively about themselves and cite a dearth of validation for their feelings and opinions as primary concerns.

Clear, consistent communication is instrumental in preventing misunderstandings and misinterpretations, ensuring that both partners are aligned and reducing the likelihood of conflict. When couples establish an environment of open communication, they create a safe space where thoughts and feelings can be freely expressed without fear of judgment or criticism.

This fosters a profound sense of understanding and connection, enabling couples to confront challenges together and fortify their relationship's resilience and strength over time.

Communication not only serves as the bridge that connects individuals but also acts as a shield against the silent killer of marriage: unexpressed expectations. Proper communication is the antidote to this insidious threat, as it leaves no room for guesswork or assumptions. Instead, it makes expectations clear and straightforward, ensuring that both partners are on the same page and working towards shared goals.

Unexpressed expectations can wreak havoc on a marriage, leading to resentment, frustration, and, ultimately, the breakdown of the relationship. When expectations are not communicated openly and honestly, misunderstandings arise, and assumptions take root. Partners may find themselves disappointed when their unspoken desires are not met, leading to feelings of neglect or betrayal.

Effective communication eliminates this risk by encouraging couples to express their needs, desires, and concerns openly. It fosters an environment where both partners feel safe and comfortable discussing their expectations without fear of judgment or reprisal. By communicating openly and honestly, couples can avoid misunderstandings and address issues before they escalate into larger conflicts.

Furthermore, proper communication allows couples to navigate challenges and disagreements with grace and understanding. Instead of resorting to silent treatment or passive-aggressive behavior, couples can engage in constructive dialogue, working together to find mutually beneficial solutions. This collaborative approach strengthens the bond between partners and reinforces their commitment to each other.

We can not finish talking about communication without mentioning the very important aspect of communication, which is Consent.

Consent in a relationship transcends mere agreement; it's about cultivating a culture of shared decision-making and mutual understanding. From the outset of a relationship, prioritize making decisions together and seeking each other's consent on matters that impact both partners. Building a strong relationship hinges on fostering consensus and finding common ground, ensuring that both individuals feel heard and valued.

Marriage is fundamentally a partnership, a collaborative effort where both partners contribute to the shared goals and aspirations of the union. During courtship, couples should begin training themselves to set goals together and work towards them, laying the groundwork for effective teamwork in marriage. Just as a successful team relies on the synergy of its members, a thriving marriage flourishes when both partners leverage their unique strengths toward common objectives.

Effective communication serves as the cornerstone of consent in marriage, enabling partners to understand each other's perspectives and make informed decisions together. It's the bridge that connects two individuals with distinct personalities and backgrounds, fostering genuine exchange and mutual understanding.

In a marriage, where personal desires are harmonized with collective goals, consent ensures that both partners are fully engaged in the decision-making process. At the heart of consent lies the recognition that decision-making is a collaborative effort, not a contest of right or wrong.

It requires ongoing communication and open dialogue, as well as a willingness to adapt to changing circumstances. By aligning concepts and actively decoding verbal and nonverbal cues, couples foster a deeper connection and shared understanding, transcending mere words. The research underscores the importance of understanding marriage commitments and each other's morals and values in preventing divorce. Building a habit of agreement, even amidst discussions, fosters mutual respect and strengthens the foundation of the relationship.

Instead of agreeing to disagree, couples should strive to find common ground and reach agreements that honor both partners' perspectives and needs. Through continuous communication and mutual consent, couples lay the groundwork for a lasting and fulfilling partnership.

In essence, communication stands as the lifeline of a thriving marriage, serving as the cornerstone for trust, intimacy, and resilience. Couples lay the groundwork for a relationship founded on understanding, respect, and unwavering support by placing a premium on open and honest communication. With clear expectations and effective communication channels in place, couples can navigate any challenge and emerge from adversity stronger and more united than ever before.

Indeed, the quality of communication within a marriage is directly proportional to the overall quality of the relationship itself. Healthy marriages flourish when communication is characterized by mutual understanding, respect, and emotional connection. By prioritizing communication and honing active listening and effective speaking skills, couples can cultivate a deeper bond, nurturing a marriage that thrives on a bedrock of love, trust, and enduring commitment.

As you've been reading through these insights, it's possible that you're reflecting on your own marital situation, perhaps feeling disheartened or considering the prospect of divorce. However, I want to urge you to pause and reconsider. While divorce might seem like the easiest way out of a challenging marriage, it's rarely the best or most cost-effective solution in the long run. The repercussions of divorce extend beyond just the spouses involved; they also impact children and have broader societal implications.

Instead of rushing into divorce, it's worth exploring ways to rebuild and strengthen your marriage. Healthy marriages serve as the backbone of families, providing a stable foundation for children to thrive. When parents maintain a positive relationship, it sets a powerful example for their children, teaching them important values like love, respect, and effective communication.

Research indicates that the quality of parental relationships directly impacts children's behavior, school performance, and overall well-being. Parental absence, whether due to divorce or other reasons, can have detrimental effects on children's behavior and mental health. Without proper guidance and supervision, children may turn to unhealthy coping mechanisms like substance abuse.

Stable and loving marriages play a crucial role in providing a nurturing environment for children's development, safeguarding their future success and well-being.

Moreover, the impact of stable marriages extends beyond the family unit to the workplace and society as a whole. Research suggests that employees' personal lives can significantly affect their job performance and interactions with colleagues. Employers have a vested interest in creating a supportive work environment that acknowledges and accommodates employees' personal challenges, including those related to marriage and family. The centrality of marriage in building stable families underscores the importance of investing in marital relationships.

Statistics reveal that children from divorced homes are more likely to experience behavioral problems, academic difficulties, and health issues. Additionally, father absence has been linked to higher rates of infant mortality and parenting stress, highlighting the vital role that fathers play in supporting their children's well-being. Furthermore, the negative health consequences of divorce are well-documented, with separated or divorced individuals facing a higher risk of mortality from various causes.

Divorce often leads to changes in health behaviors, such as smoking and excessive alcohol consumption, which further exacerbate the risk of chronic disease and premature death. Women, in particular, are disproportionately affected by divorce, experiencing financial instability and reduced earning potential.

In addition to the existing complexities surrounding divorce, recent findings from Forbes Magazine shed light on the high incidence of remarriage and subsequent divorces.

Despite the dissolution of their first marriage, a significant number of individuals—64% of men and 52% of women—choose to enter into marriage again. However, the statistics reveal a concerning trend: 67% of second marriages and 73% of third marriages end in divorce. This highlights the importance of not hastily resorting to divorce as an easy solution, as remarriage may not necessarily guarantee long-term marital success.

Moreover, a study conducted in the United Kingdom underscores the prevalence of regret among divorcees. Alarmingly, 50% of individuals who opted for divorce expressed regret over their decision. Specifically, 54% admitted to having second thoughts about the divorce, while 42% contemplated reconciling with their former partner. These findings challenge the notion that divorce offers a definitive solution to marital problems and suggest that many individuals may come to regret their decision to end their marriage.

Considering these statistics, it becomes evident that divorce is not a panacea for marital issues and may lead to unforeseen consequences. Rather than hastily pursuing divorce, couples are encouraged to explore avenues for reconciliation and seek professional assistance to address underlying issues.

By investing in their marriage and prioritizing effective communication and mutual understanding, couples can work towards building a resilient and fulfilling relationship that withstands the test of time. The repercussions of failed marriages extend far beyond the individuals directly involved, resonating throughout communities and society at large. Divorce can have profound impacts on children, leading to emotional turmoil and instability. Additionally, divorce rates have societal implications, contributing to broader social issues such as poverty and mental health challenges.

Therefore, rather than viewing divorce as a quick fix, couples should consider the long-term implications and seek support to navigate challenges within their marriage. By investing in their relationship and fostering open communication, couples can create a stable and supportive environment for themselves and their children, ultimately contributing to the well-being of society as a whole.

If you find yourself in a marriage lacking a sense of purpose or entered into out of convenience, it's crucial to recognize that there is hope for revitalizing your relationship. Rather than succumbing to feelings of despair or resignation, I recommend actively seeking ways to rediscover purpose and meaning within your marriage.

One powerful approach is to identify shared interests or goals that you and your partner can pursue together. By finding common ground and investing in activities or projects that resonate with both of you, you can reignite the spark of connection and breathe new life into your relationship. The journey of rediscovering purpose within your marriage begins with honest and open communication. Take the time to engage in heartfelt conversations with your partner about your individual aspirations, values, and desires for the future.

Listen attentively to each other's perspectives and be willing to compromise and find common ground. By fostering an environment of mutual respect and understanding, you can lay the foundation for a renewed sense of purpose and unity within your relationship. Once you've identified areas of shared interest or goals, it's essential to take proactive steps to pursue them together. Whether it's embarking on a new hobby, volunteering for a cause you both care about or setting ambitious goals for personal or professional growth, engaging in joint endeavors can help strengthen your bond and reignite the sense of purpose within your marriage.

MARRIAGE

As you work together towards common objectives, you'll not only experience a renewed sense of unity but also develop a deeper appreciation for each other's strengths and contributions. Transforming your struggling marriage into a journey of rediscovery and rejuvenation requires patience, dedication, and a willingness to embrace change.

Be open to exploring new experiences and stepping outside of your comfort zone as you navigate this journey together. Celebrate the small victories along the way and acknowledge the progress you've made together, no matter how incremental it may seem.

For a significant stretch of time, I ardently pursued my passion for leadership development, hoping to ignite a similar enthusiasm in my wife. Yet, despite my best efforts, I encountered resistance. It wasn't until I had a profound realization that leadership extends far beyond the boardroom—it emanates from the very heart of a relationship—that I found the key to unlocking a deeper connection with my spouse.

In my journey, I came to understand that true leadership begins within the confines of our home, within the intimate spaces of our relationship; as my mentor used to say, you can only lead from your bedroom. It dawned on me that my attempts to sway my wife toward my passion were well-intentioned but misguided. I wasn't necessarily on the wrong path, but I wasn't fully aligned with what truly mattered in our shared journey.

By shifting my focus towards something that resonated with both of us—nurturing and strengthening marriages and relationships—I discovered a newfound sense of purpose and unity.

Instead of persisting in a solitary pursuit, I learned the value of collaboration and shared aspirations. Together, we embarked on a journey to build something meaningful, something that reflected our combined vision and values. This transformation taught me a profound lesson: it's not about being right or wrong; it's about finding common ground and pursuing endeavors that speak to both partners' interests and passions.

By identifying activities or causes that ignite mutual excitement and engagement, couples can foster deeper connections and cultivate a shared sense of purpose. As we ventured into this collaborative endeavor, I witnessed the power of partnership in action. Our shared project became a catalyst for growth, not only in our relationship but also in our individual lives. It provided a platform for us to blend our unique talents and perspectives, creating something far more impactful than either of us could have achieved alone.

Ultimately, our journey taught us that the most fulfilling relationships are those where both partners feel seen, heard, and valued. By prioritizing shared interests and pursuits, couples can forge a bond that transcends individual differences and flourishes in the light of mutual understanding and support.

In addition to pursuing shared interests and goals, consider seeking guidance from a qualified therapist or counselor who can provide valuable insights and support as you work to revitalize your relationship. Professional counseling can offer a safe and supportive space for exploring underlying issues, improving communication skills, and developing strategies for overcoming challenges.

Ultimately, by investing in your marriage and prioritizing shared purpose and meaning, you can transform your struggling relationship into a source of renewed love, connection, and fulfillment. Embrace the opportunity to embark on this journey of rediscovery together, knowing that with dedication and effort, you can build a stronger, more resilient partnership that stands the test of time.

One of the most significant hurdles to effective communication in relationships is often the lack of deep familiarity and understanding between partners. Have you ever wondered why your spouse seems to effortlessly engage in conversations with others yet struggles to communicate with you? It could be that your spouse simply doesn't feel they know enough about you to engage in meaningful discussions.

Consider this: Do you know what truly matters to your partner? Have you taken the time to understand their interests, passions, and aspirations? Similarly, does your partner know what keeps you up at night or your deepest hopes and dreams? True communication involves more than just exchanging words—it's about connecting on a deeper level and understanding each other's innermost thoughts and feelings.

Creating a conducive environment for communication is crucial in fostering a deeper connection with your partner. Don't expect communication to just happen; actively cultivate opportunities for open and honest dialogue. Schedule regular date nights or check-in trips where you and your spouse can focus solely on each other and catch up on what's happening in your lives. Be genuinely interested in what your spouse is doing, even if it's challenging for them to open up initially.

Show empathy, patience, and understanding, and gradually, they'll feel more comfortable sharing their thoughts and feelings with you. Communication thrives on mutual understanding and empathy, and the key to achieving this is through active engagement and genuine interest in each other's lives. By taking the time to truly know and understand your partner, you can overcome communication barriers and build a stronger, more resilient relationship based on trust, respect, and mutual support.

When communication hits a roadblock, and you're unsure where to begin, consider revisiting the conversations and activities that initially brought you together. Think back to those early days of your relationship—what were the topics you talked about most? What activities did you enjoy together? Chances are, these shared interests and meaningful conversations played a significant role in forming the foundation of your bond.

These discussions likely sparked a sense of connection and excitement, laying the groundwork for your relationship. Rekindle the magic of those early conversations by intentionally reintroducing the activities that meant a lot to both of you. Whether it's revisiting favorite date spots, reminiscing about cherished memories, or engaging in shared hobbies, these experiences can reignite the spark of connection and remind you of what initially drew you together. By intentionally nurturing the activities and conversations that brought you closer as a couple, you can breathe new life into your relationship and reignite the flame of communication. Embrace the opportunity to rediscover each other and strengthen your bond, building a foundation of trust, understanding, and shared experiences that will sustain your relationship for years to come.

MARRIAGE

"Communication" is the foundation of any healthy relationship, and it is especially crucial during the power struggle stage. Couples need to be able to communicate openly, honestly, and respectfully with each other, even when it is difficult. This involves sharing their feelings, needs, and expectations in a way that is clear and constructive. Active listening is also essential, as it allows couples to truly understand each other's perspectives and build empathy.

In my own experience, communication has always been the cornerstone of my relationship with my wife. Despite living on different continents with a significant time difference, we prioritized spending hours talking on the phone every day. Those conversations were our lifeline, providing a window into each other's worlds and fostering a deep sense of connection. However, like many couples, we faced challenges that tested our communication when setbacks arose, and we lost one another. It became clear that maintaining open and intentional communication required effort and dedication.

I realized that I couldn't take our communication for granted; I had to carve out time in my day to ensure that we could continue sharing our thoughts, feelings, and experiences. Recognizing that each couple has their own unique dynamics and interests, my wife and I discovered a simple yet effective way to nurture our connection. While I enjoy playing tennis, my wife finds solace in walking. Rather than letting these differences create distance between us, we found a compromise that works for both of us. After my tennis practice, my wife joins me for the walk home, providing us with uninterrupted time to talk and reconnect. This ritual has become invaluable to us, offering a sacred space where we can communicate openly and honestly without distractions. This experience taught me the importance of finding what works for you as a couple and prioritizing your relationship above all else. Your marriage is a precious asset that deserves your attention and effort.

By recommitting to your relationship and nurturing open dialogue, you can embark on a journey to rebuild a sense of purpose and connection. It's important to acknowledge that every relationship faces challenges, but with dedication and effort, you can overcome obstacles and cultivate a deeply fulfilling partnership. Take the time to reflect on what drew you together in the first place and rediscover the shared goals and dreams that brought meaning to your relationship. Prioritize honest communication, actively listening to each other's needs and concerns, and fostering an environment where both partners feel heard and valued. Remember, rebuilding a relationship takes time and patience, but by working together with love and commitment, you can create a stronger, more resilient bond that withstands the test of time.

By investing in effective communication, shared activities, and mutual understanding, you can strengthen the foundation of your relationship and overcome any obstacles that come your way. Couples can deepen their bond, reaffirm their dedication to each other by focusing on the three Cs- common goals, commitment, and communication- and cultivate a shared vision for the future.

Together, you can conquer challenges, celebrate victories, and create a life filled with love, joy, and fulfillment. With dedication and perseverance, nothing will stand in the way of your happiness and success as a couple.

To the survivors of the 94 genocide against the Tutsi who are embarking on the challenging journey of rebuilding their marriages, I offer words of compassion, resilience, and hope. The trauma and loss experienced during such horrific events can profoundly impact relationships, but it's important to remember that healing and restoration are possible. Honor the journey you've traveled and acknowledge the strength it took to endure such unimaginable pain.

Recognize that rebuilding a marriage after such trauma requires time, patience, and support.

Seek out professional counseling or therapy tailored to the unique challenges faced by survivors of genocide, providing a safe space to process emotions, navigate complex grief, and learn healthy communication skills. Cultivate a spirit of forgiveness, both towards your partner and yourself, as releasing resentment and embracing empathy can pave the way for healing and reconciliation.

Focus on rebuilding trust and intimacy through small acts of kindness, understanding, and vulnerability, sharing your experiences openly with your partner to foster a deeper sense of connection. Engage in activities that bring joy and fulfillment as a couple, whether exploring new hobbies or spending time in nature. Remember, rebuilding a marriage is a journey, not a destination, so be patient with yourselves and each other, celebrating the progress made along the way.

With determination, love, and support, you can create a marriage that honors your resilience and embodies hope for a brighter future.

CHAPTER 5
CULTIVATING TRUST IN FRIENDSHIPS

Rebuilding trust in humanity and forming meaningful friendships. Nurturing connections based on empathy, understanding, and shared experiences.

The aftermath of the genocide against the Tutsi in Rwanda left a profound impact on the trust between individuals, extending beyond familial relationships to deeply affect friendships.

Before delving into the nuances of rebuilding friendships in the aftermath of trauma, it's crucial to understand the essence of friendship and its profound impact on our lives. By exploring what friendship truly entails and why it holds such importance, we gain a deeper appreciation for the journey of rebuilding trust and connection in the wake of adversity. So, let's embark on this exploration together, unraveling the layers of friendship and discovering the transformative power it holds in our lives.

Friendship is a cornerstone of human connection, an intricate tapestry woven with threads of trust, empathy, and mutual support. It serves as a beacon of light in life's darkest moments and a source of joy during times of celebration. However, the significance of friendship extends beyond mere companionship; it plays a vital role in our emotional well-being and personal growth.

Friendship is not merely a casual connection; it's a profound bond built on trust, empathy, and mutual understanding. At its core, friendship represents a commitment to support and uplift one another through life's trials and triumphs. This mutual agreement to stand by each other's side, whether spoken or unspoken, forms the foundation of authentic friendship.

The power of choice underscores the significance of friendship in all relationships, emphasizing the importance of reciprocity and mutual respect.

While we may not choose our family members, for a family to stand, we do have to choose our family members to treat them as family, highlighting the transformative nature of choice in relationships. In the relationship with oneself, cultivating self-compassion and self-awareness is akin to being one's own best friend. In marital unions, the strongest bonds are rooted in authentic friendship, where spouses serve as each other's confidants and champions. Even in professional settings, elements of friendship are essential for collaboration and effectiveness. Acquaintances evolve into friendships through shared experiences and genuine connection, demonstrating the dynamic nature of human relationships.

Trust serves as the cornerstone of friendship, fostering an environment where individuals can be vulnerable and authentic without fear of judgment. True friends offer unwavering support, celebrating each other's successes and providing comfort during difficult times. The essence of friendship transcends boundaries, enriching all aspects of our lives and relationships. The significance of friendships extends far beyond companionship; they play a pivotal role in personal growth and well-being.

Friends challenge us to step outside of our comfort zones, offering new perspectives and experiences that broaden our horizons. They provide invaluable support during life's challenges, serving as pillars of strength and sources of encouragement. Research has shown that individuals with strong social networks experience greater happiness and resilience in the face of adversity.

In essence, friendships are a source of joy, connection, and fulfillment in our lives. They provide a sense of belonging and purpose, enriching our experiences and helping us navigate life's journey with grace and resilience. As we explore the dynamics of rebuilding trust and friendship in the aftermath of trauma, it's essential to recognize the profound impact that genuine connections have on our well-being and growth. Remember that Life travels at the speed of relationships.

Having recognized and established the pivotal role friendships play in shaping our interpersonal connections, as a bedrock of all other relationships permeating every facet of our social interaction, let's delve deeper into some guiding principles that underpin meaningful and robust friendships.

The principles governing friendships are universal, transcending the boundaries of familial, romantic, or professional connections.

Therefore, the values and behaviors we uphold in our friendships reverberate throughout all aspects of our lives, shaping our character and influencing our interactions with others.

One fundamental aspect of friendship is the sacred trust shared between friends, encapsulated in the commitment to safeguard each other's confidences. True friends understand the importance of privacy and discretion, honoring the sanctity of their bond by keeping secrets entrusted to them. It's a betrayal of trust when one breaches this pact of confidentiality, often resulting in irreparable damage to the friendship.

Integrity forms another cornerstone of genuine friendship, wherein individuals uphold their own values while respecting those of their friends. This entails a willingness to engage in open dialogue, embracing diverse perspectives, and aligning actions with deeply held principles. The adage "bad company corrupts character" underscores the significance of surrounding oneself with friends who uphold similar values, fostering an environment conducive to personal growth and moral integrity.

Honesty serves as the lifeblood of authentic friendships, fostering transparency and vulnerability in interpersonal interactions. Friends must feel safe to express themselves openly, even when discussions delve into sensitive or challenging topics. It's through candid conversations that trust deepens, laying the foundation for enduring bonds forged in mutual respect and understanding.

Empathy, a hallmark of meaningful friendships, entails the ability to empathize with a friend's experiences and emotions.

It requires actively listening, offering support, and validating their feelings without judgment. Empathetic friends create a safe space for vulnerability, nurturing an environment where individuals feel seen, heard, and valued.

Support and celebration are essential components of nurturing friendships, serving as pillars of strength during both triumphs and tribulations. True friends stand by each other's side, offering unwavering support during times of adversity and rejoicing in each other's successes. Shared laughter, shared tears, and shared experiences deepen the bonds of friendship, fostering a sense of belonging and camaraderie.

Furthermore, genuine friendships spur personal growth by challenging individuals to aspire to greatness. Friends serve as catalysts for self-improvement, encouraging each other to step outside their comfort zones and pursue their dreams. Constructive feedback, encouragement, and accountability foster a culture of continuous learning and development, empowering individuals to reach their full potential.

In essence, the principles governing friendships are not merely confined to the realm of social interactions but permeate every sphere of human relationships. By embracing the values of trust, integrity, honesty, empathy, support, celebration, and growth, individuals cultivate rich and meaningful connections that enrich their lives and empower them to navigate the complexities of the human experience.

But, in a society where neighbors once shared bonds of camaraderie and mutual support, the horrors of the genocide shattered these connections, leaving behind a landscape of broken trust and fractured friendships.

The betrayal experienced during this dark period, where individuals turned against one another, whether out of fear, coercion, or indoctrination, inflicted deep wounds on the collective psyche of the nation. Neighbors, who were once considered friends and allies, became adversaries, perpetrating unspeakable acts of violence against others.

The sense of betrayal was particularly acute for those who sought refuge in the homes of their neighbors, only to be met with rejection and abandonment. In some tragic instances, the bonds of friendship were severed irreparably as parents sometimes even participated in the killing of their own or their friends' children. The erosion of trust that occurred during the genocide continues to reverberate through Rwandan society, undermining the foundation upon which friendships are built.

The trauma of betrayal and loss inflicted deep scars on the collective consciousness, leaving individuals wary of forming meaningful connections with others. The fear of vulnerability, coupled with the lingering specter of past betrayals, creates a pervasive sense of mistrust that permeates interpersonal relationships.

Rebuilding trust in humanity and nurturing meaningful friendships in the aftermath of such profound trauma is a daunting task. It requires individuals to confront their deepest fears and insecurities, to acknowledge the pain and betrayal they have experienced, and to cultivate empathy and understanding for others who may share similar wounds. It is a process that unfolds slowly, often marked by setbacks and challenges along the way.

However, it is also a journey of healing and reconciliation, where individuals have the opportunity to transcend the divisions of the past and forge new connections based on empathy, compassion, and shared humanity. By extending grace to one another, listening with open hearts and minds, and choosing to see the inherent worth and dignity in every individual, Rwandans can begin to rebuild the trust that was shattered by the 94 genocide against the Tutsi and nurture friendships that are grounded in mutual respect and understanding.

The journey of rebuilding trust in humanity after the profound devastation of the genocide against the Tutsi begins with a recognition of the resilience and goodness that still exist within the human spirit. While the genocide inflicted unimaginable horrors and shattered trust on a massive scale, there are also countless stories of bravery, compassion, and selflessness that emerged from the darkness. These stories serve as beacons of hope, reminding us that even in the darkest of times, there are individuals who are willing to risk their own lives to save others, to offer refuge and assistance to those in need, and to stand up against injustice and hatred.

As we embark on this journey of rebuilding trust, it is essential to acknowledge and honor these stories of courage and compassion. They remind us that despite the existence of evil and cruelty in the world, there is also immense goodness and kindness. By amplifying these stories and celebrating the individuals who embody the best of humanity, we can inspire others to follow in their footsteps and cultivate a culture of trust and solidarity.

Furthermore, the journey of rebuilding trust begins with each of us committing to being the change we wish to see in the world. It is easy to become disillusioned and cynical in the face of widespread distrust and division, but we must resist the temptation to succumb to despair.

Instead, we must strive to embody the values of empathy, compassion, and integrity in our daily lives, treating others with the same kindness and respect that we ourselves desire. This means being mindful of our words and actions and striving to uplift and support those around us. It means reaching out to lend a helping hand to those in need, even when it may be inconvenient or uncomfortable. It means standing up against injustice and discrimination and advocating for the rights and dignity of all people, regardless of their background or beliefs.

Ultimately, rebuilding trust in humanity is a collective endeavor that requires the participation and commitment of each individual. It requires us to look beyond our differences and recognize our shared humanity. It requires us to cultivate empathy and understanding for others and extend grace and forgiveness to those who may have wronged us in the past. By embracing these principles and embodying these values in our daily lives, we can contribute to the gradual restoration of trust and solidarity within our communities and society as a whole.

Though the journey may be long and challenging, it is also filled with opportunities for growth, healing, and renewal. And by walking this path together, hand in hand, we can create a brighter and more hopeful future for generations to come.

Rebuilding and nurturing trust and friendship begins with a personal commitment to cultivating integrity within ourselves. Integrity is the cornerstone of trustworthiness, reflecting a deep alignment between our thoughts, words, and actions. When we say what we mean and mean what we say, we become integrated beings, consistent and reliable in our interactions with others.

This inner consistency not only fosters trust but also serves as a reflection of our self-perception.

Our relationships with others are a mirror of our relationship with ourselves; we cannot expect others to value us more than we value ourselves or to treat us better than we treat ourselves and those around us. Maintaining integrity means honoring our word and keeping our promises. Countless relationships falter because individuals fail to uphold their commitments, eroding trust and damaging their credibility. When we break our word, we not only betray the trust of others but also compromise our own integrity.

Integrity requires a steadfast commitment to our values, which serve as our moral compass and guide our actions and decisions. Our values are the essence of who we are, springing from our deepest beliefs and convictions. Living in alignment with our values not only fosters authenticity but also sets a powerful example for others. By allowing our values to guide our actions and decisions, we demonstrate our commitment to what truly matters to us and inspire others to do the same.

However, to maintain the integrity of our values, we must wholeheartedly believe in them and be willing to stand up for them, even in the face of adversity. While our values may be deeply personal, they are not meant to be kept private. They shape not only our individual lives but also the way others perceive us.

As parents, living according to our values sets a lasting example for our children, shaping their beliefs and influencing their behavior long after we are gone. Our values become our legacy, a testament to the principles we held dear and the way we lived our lives. It's important to remember that actions speak louder than words.

Even if we espouse certain values, it is our actions that truly reflect our character. If our actions are inconsistent with our professed values, we undermine our integrity and erode trust in our relationships.

Living with integrity is not just about doing what is right for ourselves; it's about leaving a legacy of honor and integrity that will inspire and empower those who come after us. As Dr. Myles Munroe, my late mentor, once said, living with integrity is not just for ourselves but for the legacy we leave behind. Our values and the way we live our lives will shape the perceptions and experiences of those who follow in our footsteps, leaving an indelible mark on the world.

Becoming an embodiment of trust is not merely about expecting others to be trustworthy but about leading by example through our own actions and behaviors. Trust is not something that can be demanded or imposed upon others; it must be earned through consistent and authentic interactions. By demonstrating integrity, honesty, and reliability in our own words and deeds, we set the standard for trustworthiness and create an environment where trust can flourish.

To expect trust from others without embodying it ourselves is hypocritical and unfair. We cannot demand from others what we are not willing to give or demonstrate in our own lives. Trust is a reciprocal relationship that requires mutual respect, honesty, and vulnerability. By investing in our own character development and continually striving to uphold the values of trust and integrity, we pave the way for meaningful connections and genuine relationships.

Furthermore, cultivating trust within ourselves allows us to extend grace and understanding to others when they fall short.

Recognizing our own struggles and imperfections enables us to empathize with the challenges faced by others and offer support and encouragement rather than judgment or condemnation. Just as we seek understanding and forgiveness for our own shortcomings, we can extend the same compassion to those around us, fostering a culture of acceptance and growth.

Ultimately, becoming an embodiment of trust requires a commitment to personal growth and self-awareness. It involves acknowledging our own limitations and areas for improvement while striving to live in alignment with our values and principles. By embodying trust in our words, actions, and relationships, we not only inspire confidence and loyalty in others but also contribute to the creation of a more trustworthy and compassionate world.

I cannot continue talking about trust without touching on one of the biggest problems in our culture and how it impacts ways of relating to one another: the Silent killer of many relationships: unexpressed expectations.

Unexpressed expectations are a silent killer of trust within friendships, often leading to misunderstandings and feelings of betrayal. When we fail to communicate our needs, desires, and boundaries clearly, we set the stage for disappointment and resentment. Expecting our friends to intuitively understand our unspoken wishes is both unrealistic and unfair.

Instead, integrity demands that we express ourselves openly and honestly, ensuring that our intentions and expectations are transparent to those around us. By practicing clear and effective communication, we empower ourselves and our friends to navigate friendships with clarity and mutual understanding.

Effective communication is the bedrock of healthy friendships, providing the framework for expressing expectations and resolving conflicts.

Active listening and articulate expression enable friends to communicate their needs and desires effectively, fostering a sense of connection and camaraderie. When we openly communicate our expectations, we create an environment where both parties feel heard, valued, and respected. By prioritizing open and honest communication, we lay the groundwork for building trust and strengthening our friendships.

The misconception that true friendship entails mind-reading is a fallacy that undermines the foundation of healthy relationships. Expecting our friends to anticipate our needs without verbalizing them sets an unrealistic standard and breeds resentment when our unspoken desires go unfulfilled. In reality, healthy friendships are built on mutual understanding, empathy, and effective communication. By verbalizing our expectations and desires, we empower our friends to support and uplift us in ways that align with our needs and preferences. Clear communication fosters trust and intimacy, allowing friendships to flourish and thrive.

Establishing clear expectations in friendships is essential for fostering mutual support and accountability. When both parties understand their roles and responsibilities within the friendship, they can work together to nurture and sustain it. Clear expectations provide a roadmap for navigating challenges and conflicts, enabling friends to address issues proactively and collaboratively. By fostering mutual respect and understanding, clear expectations lay the groundwork for building trust and fostering healthy, fulfilling friendships.

Mutual respect is the cornerstone of healthy friendships, providing the foundation for trust, communication, and camaraderie. When we respect our friends, we acknowledge their inherent worth and value, valuing their opinions, feelings, and boundaries. Mutual respect creates a safe and supportive environment where individuals feel empowered to express themselves authentically and without fear of judgment or criticism. By prioritizing mutual respect in our friendships, we cultivate trust, understanding, and emotional connection, laying the groundwork for lasting and meaningful bonds.

As we wrap up this chapter, it's important to reflect on the key takeaway: rebuilding trust and friendship after trauma is a nuanced journey that demands patience, empathy, and intentional dedication. This journey requires a deep commitment from all parties involved, as it involves navigating complex emotions and experiences.

Acknowledging the impact of the trauma is the first step towards healing. It's essential to recognize that the traumatic experience has profoundly affected the dynamics of the relationship, potentially straining or fracturing trust. Both you and your friends may carry emotional scars from the trauma, which can influence your interactions and communication.

Creating a safe space for open and honest communication is paramount in rebuilding trust and friendship. Encourage your friends to express their feelings and concerns without fear of judgment, and reciprocate by sharing your own emotions and experiences related to the trauma.

Effective communication fosters understanding and empathy, allowing both parties to validate each other's perspectives and feelings.

Practicing empathy and compassion is crucial in supporting your friends through their healing journey. Show genuine empathy towards their experiences and emotions, seeking to understand their perspective without minimizing or dismissing their feelings. Offer unconditional support and reassurance, demonstrating that you are there for them in their time of need.

Establishing clear boundaries within the relationship is essential for creating a sense of safety and trust. Respect each other's boundaries and communicate openly about your needs and limits. Boundaries help maintain healthy dynamics and prevent further harm, allowing both parties to feel secure and respected in the relationship.

Taking small steps toward rebuilding trust is key to the healing process. Start by demonstrating reliability and consistency in your actions, such as keeping your promises and prioritizing honesty and transparency. Building trust takes time and patience, so be prepared for setbacks and challenges along the way.

Seeking professional support from a therapist or counselor can provide invaluable guidance and tools for navigating the complexities of rebuilding trust and friendship after trauma. A trained professional can offer insights and strategies tailored to your specific needs, facilitating healing and growth in the relationship.

Practicing self-care is essential for your own well-being as you support your friend through their healing journey. Prioritize activities that promote relaxation, stress relief, and emotional well-being, ensuring that you are taking care of yourself emotionally, mentally, and physically.

Above all, approach the process with patience, understanding, and resilience. Rebuilding trust and friendship after trauma is a gradual and nonlinear process that requires commitment and effort from both parties. By prioritizing open communication, empathy, mutual respect, and self-care, relationships can emerge stronger and more resilient than before, fostering healing and growth for all involve

CHAPTER 6

BALANCING PERSONAL AND PROFESSIONAL LIFE

Professional relationships are the cornerstone of success in the workplace, encompassing connections and collaborations driven by shared objectives and mutual respect. Unlike personal relationships, which may evolve over time, professional connections are often formalized from the outset through written agreements or contracts founded on a clear understanding of expectations and responsibilities, establishing a framework for collaboration and growth. These agreements outline the terms of engagement, ensuring clarity and accountability for both parties involved. In Rwanda, labor laws mandate that unwritten employment contracts cannot exceed ninety consecutive days, emphasizing the importance of formalizing professional agreements. Similarly, in the United States, verbal contracts are restricted in duration and scope to protect the interests of all parties involved.

Recognizing that professional relationships are dynamic entities that require active maintenance and nurturing is essential. While they may begin with a formal agreement, such as an employment contract, their longevity and effectiveness depend on ongoing communication and mutual support.

In many ways, professional relationships represent a delicate balance between give and take, requiring both parties to contribute to their development and sustainability.

Unlike personal relationships, where emotions and familiarity often dictate interactions, professional connections thrive on clarity, transparency, and accountability. Establishing boundaries and expectations early on is crucial for maintaining professionalism and ensuring that both parties uphold their commitments. The significance of professional relationships cannot be overstated, particularly in the context of career advancement and business success.

These connections are conduits for knowledge exchange, networking opportunities, and skill development. A robust professional network can open doors to new career opportunities, foster project collaboration, and enhance overall job satisfaction.

Moreover, effective professional relationships contribute to increased productivity and efficiency in the workplace, as colleagues and partners leverage each other's expertise and resources to achieve common goals. Furthermore, formalizing professional agreements through written contracts or agreements is essential for delineating roles, responsibilities, and expectations.

Legal frameworks, such as employment laws and contractual regulations, provide a foundation for ensuring fairness and accountability in professional relationships.

By adhering to these guidelines, individuals and organizations can mitigate the risk of disputes or misunderstandings and foster an environment of trust and reliability. Cultivating and maintaining professional relationships extends beyond individual success to broader organizational and societal benefits in today's interconnected world.

Collaborative partnerships and networks drive innovation, economic growth, and social progress, creating opportunities for individuals and communities to thrive.

As such, investing in the development of strong professional connections is not only beneficial on a personal level but also contributes to the collective advancement of society.

The aftermath of the 94 genocide against the Tutsi in Rwanda had far-reaching effects, extending into various aspects of society, including the professional realm. The repercussions of this dark chapter in history could have significantly impacted the merit-based hiring process, ideally guided solely by an individual's qualifications and ability to meet business needs.

However, the deep-seated divisions resulting from the genocide may have clouded judgment, potentially leading to biases and discriminatory practices in hiring and forming partnerships. If present, this bias could compromise the integrity of the hiring process, unfairly judging individuals based on their background rather than their skills and qualifications.

This scenario undermines the fundamental principles of fairness and equal opportunity, hindering economic growth and development. Moreover, prevalent biases related to one's background in the professional realm could inhibit partnership formation and business establishment. Collaboration becomes notably challenging when individuals hail from different sides of the historical divide, where trust and mutual respect may be lacking.

The lingering effects of the genocide may contribute to a lack of cohesion and unity, further exacerbating social tensions and divisions within post-genocide Rwanda. These divisions impede economic progress and perpetuate social fragmentation, posing obstacles to the country's overall stability and development.

To surmount these barriers, prioritizing efforts to foster inclusivity, promote meritocracy, and address underlying prejudices that impede professional relationships is essential. Embracing diversity and confronting the legacies of the past are crucial steps toward building a more equitable and prosperous future for Rwanda.

By creating a culture of inclusivity and meritocracy, where individuals are judged based on skills and qualifications rather than background, Rwanda can unlock its full potential and create opportunities for all its citizens.

Additionally, addressing the root causes of prejudice and discrimination necessitates ongoing education, awareness-building, and dialogue within society. Rwanda's strength lies in the diversity of its citizens, and by harnessing these talents, skills, and perspectives, the nation can build a resilient and thriving economy that benefits everyone.

All stakeholders must work together to achieve the vision of a united and prosperous Rwanda, where every individual has the opportunity to contribute and thrive.

PROFESSIONAL LIFE

Personal trauma, whether stemming from past experiences or recent events, can profoundly impact an individual's professional and work life, creating significant challenges in maintaining a healthy work-life balance and performing effectively in professional settings. Symptoms of trauma, such as anxiety, depression, post-traumatic stress disorder (PTSD), and emotional distress, can impede one's capacity to focus, make decisions, and engage in productive work-related activities.

These challenges may manifest in decreased productivity, difficulty concentrating, and impaired interpersonal relationships, making it challenging for individuals to maintain their usual level of performance or collaborate effectively with colleagues. Moreover, trauma can disrupt work-life balance, draining individuals of emotional and mental energy and leaving them feeling exhausted and overwhelmed. Coping with trauma requires significant resources, leaving little room for leisure activities, social connections, or personal responsibilities outside of work. Despite these challenges, individuals can employ various strategies to navigate the impact of trauma on their professional and work life effectively.

Seeking support from mental health professionals or support groups can provide valuable resources and coping mechanisms for managing trauma-related symptoms. Therapy, counseling, or peer support can offer a safe space to process emotions, develop healthy coping strategies, and build resilience.

Establishing clear boundaries between work and personal life is essential for maintaining balance and preventing burnout. Setting aside dedicated time for self-care activities, relaxation, and leisure pursuits can help individuals recharge and enhance overall well-being.

Cultivating a supportive work environment that prioritizes employee well-being and mental health is crucial for individuals navigating trauma.

Employers can implement policies and practices that promote flexibility, provide access to mental health resources, and foster a culture of empathy and understanding.

Open communication channels and opportunities for feedback can help employees feel valued and supported in the workplace.

Additionally, individuals can focus on professional growth and development to reclaim agency and purpose in the aftermath of trauma. Setting realistic goals, seeking opportunities for skill development, and pursuing meaningful projects can instill a sense of accomplishment and progress. By focusing on personal and professional growth, individuals can reclaim control and agency in their lives, empowering them to move forward and thrive despite past challenges.

Furthermore, the trauma of events like the 94 genocide against the Tutsi undoubtedly had profound effects on the professional relationships of survivors. Interpersonal dynamics and trust issues may have been affected, making it challenging to form meaningful connections and navigate workplace interactions effectively. Heightened sensitivity to discrimination or bias could have also led to conflicts or strained relationships in the workplace.

To overcome these effects, prioritizing healing and creating supportive environments is crucial. Trauma-informed policies and practices and a supportive workplace culture can provide survivors with the necessary support and accommodations. Providing trauma-informed training and encouraging self-care and resilience can further aid in mitigating the impact of trauma on professional relationships.

By addressing the effects of trauma and implementing trauma-informed practices, employers can create environments where survivors feel supported, valued, and able to thrive in their careers.

This holistic approach fosters a workplace culture of empathy, understanding, and inclusivity, ultimately contributing to the well-being and success of all employees.

Navigating the complexities of professional relationships requires more than just technical skills and expertise; it demands a deep understanding of fundamental principles that govern effective collaboration, communication, and conduct in the workplace.

Establishing and upholding good workplace practices that facilitate growth, well-being, and success is crucial to ensuring that professional relationships remain truly professional.

This guide explores the essential principles for fostering healthy and productive professional relationships, from establishing clear contracts and boundaries to prioritizing transparency, communication, and professionalism. These principles serve as guiding beacons for individuals and organizations striving for excellence in their interactions and endeavors.

By embracing these principles, professionals can cultivate trust, foster collaboration, and drive success in today's dynamic and interconnected business landscape. Join us as we delve into the foundational pillars of healthy professional relationships and discover how they can transform how we work and thrive in the modern world.

Here are some of these principles for Healthy Professional Relationships:

Contracts and Agreements: Formalizing professional relationships through written contracts is not just a formality but a necessity. These documents outline expectations, deliverables, and timelines, protecting all parties involved and preventing disputes down the line. While trust is crucial in any relationship, relying solely on trust or emotions in professional matters can lead to misunderstandings and complications. A professional relationship should always be defined and governed by a contract, ensuring clarity, accountability, and legal protection for everyone involved. Despite cultural aversions to formal contracts, especially in certain communities, understanding the importance of clear agreements can save individuals from headaches, hassles, and even heartbreaks in the long run. When engaging in professional endeavors, viewing interactions through the lens of contracts and agreements helps maintain professionalism and clarity, ensuring that all parties understand their roles and responsibilities.

Clarity and Boundaries: Clearly defining the nature and purpose of professional relationships is essential to prevent misunderstandings and maintain professionalism. Establishing clear boundaries ensures that interactions remain focused on work-related matters and prevents personal dynamics from interfering with professional objectives. While it's natural to have friendly interactions with colleagues, maintaining a professional demeanor is crucial, particularly in business settings. Drawing a clear line between personal and professional relationships helps individuals navigate professional challenges and maintain respect and professionalism in their interactions. Without clearly defined boundaries, professional relationships can become blurred, leading to confusion, conflicts, and compromised outcomes.

Merit and Qualification: Base professional relationships on merit and qualifications rather than personal connections or affiliations. Collaborate with individuals based on their competence and expertise relevant to the task at hand, ensuring the best outcomes for all involved. While personal relationships may foster trust and rapport, they should not overshadow the importance of meritocracy in professional settings. Hiring or partnering with individuals solely based on personal relationships can undermine the integrity of the business and compromise its success. Conversely, overlooking qualified candidates or collaborators due to personal biases or preferences is equally detrimental. Striking a balance between personal connections and professional qualifications is crucial in fostering productive and successful professional relationships.

Transparency and Communication: Foster open and honest communication in professional relationships, addressing issues or concerns promptly and directly to maintain trust and collaboration. Effective communication is the cornerstone of healthy professional relationships, facilitating transparency, clarity, and alignment of goals. When issues arise, addressing them openly and directly prevents misunderstandings and resentment from festering, fostering a culture of trust and accountability. Transparency in communication builds confidence and strengthens relationships, enabling individuals to navigate challenges and conflicts constructively. By prioritizing open communication and transparency, professionals can foster positive working relationships built on mutual respect and understanding.

Professional Conduct: Maintain professionalism at all times, demonstrating respect, integrity, and courtesy in all interactions and decisions. Professional conduct entails separating personal emotions from business dealings, making decisions based on merit and objectivity rather than personal biases or preferences.

While personal relationships may exist outside of professional contexts, maintaining professionalism requires individuals to prioritize business objectives and uphold ethical standards. Treating colleagues, clients, and partners with respect and courtesy fosters a conducive work environment and enhances collaboration and productivity. By adhering to professional standards of conduct, individuals contribute to a culture of professionalism and integrity in their organizations and industries.

Exceed Expectations: Strive to exceed expectations in all professional endeavors, going above and beyond to deliver exceptional results and create value. Whether as an employee, entrepreneur, or service provider, consistently surpassing expectations sets individuals apart and fosters long-term success and growth. Instead of merely meeting contractual obligations, seek opportunities to add value, innovate, and exceed client or employer expectations. By consistently delivering more than expected, individuals not only enhance their reputation and credibility but also lay the groundwork for future opportunities and success. Investing in excellence and continuous improvement positions professionals for long-term growth and fulfillment, ensuring their contributions are valued and recognized in the marketplace.

In conclusion, adhering to these principles fosters healthy and productive professional relationships, enabling individuals and organizations to thrive in an increasingly competitive and interconnected world. By prioritizing clarity, transparency, professionalism, and excellence in their interactions and conduct, professionals can build trust, drive collaboration, and achieve meaningful results in their respective fields. As Rwanda works towards its vision of becoming a self-sufficient and prosperous nation, embracing these principles can contribute to the collective strength and resilience of its workforce, paving the way for sustainable growth and development.

CHAPTER 7
BUILDING POSITIVE ACQUAINTANCESHIPS

Overcoming barriers to connecting with others and forming acquaintanceships. Fostering a positive outlook on human relationships and interactions.

Acquaintances are individuals with whom you share some familiarity or interaction but have yet to develop a close or intimate relationship. These connections can be formed through various avenues, such as work, school, social gatherings, or online platforms, where brief encounters or exchanges of words initiate the acquaintance.

From casual encounters to more extended interactions, acquaintances form a spectrum of relationships that bridge the gap between strangers and close companions. The importance of acquaintances lies in their potential to evolve into meaningful connections that extend beyond the initial introduction. While they may not be as significant as close friends or family members, acquaintances are gateways to new relationships, experiences, and perspectives.

Every profound friendship or partnership begins with an initial acquaintance, emphasizing the significance of these initial interactions. Thus, nurturing these budding relationships with care and consideration is essential, as they lay the foundation for future connections and opportunities. Beyond facilitating the formation of new relationships, acquaintances offer a myriad of benefits that contribute to personal growth and enrichment.

Firstly, they introduce us to new experiences and opportunities we may not have encountered otherwise. Whether it's an invitation to a social event or participation in a shared activity, acquaintances expand our horizons and expose us to diverse aspects of life.

Moreover, acquaintances bring fresh perspectives and insights that challenge our existing beliefs and broaden our worldview. Through interactions with individuals from different backgrounds and experiences, we gain valuable insights into alternative ways of thinking and living. This diversity of perspectives fosters intellectual curiosity and encourages continuous learning and self-reflection.

While acquaintances may not offer the same level of emotional support or intimacy as close relationships, they nonetheless play a significant role in our social landscape. They provide companionship and camaraderie in various contexts, contributing to our well-being and sense of belonging.

By acknowledging and appreciating the value of acquaintanceships, we cultivate a more inclusive and interconnected social network that enriches our lives in myriad ways.

The impact of the genocide against the Tutsi on relationships extended far beyond immediate family and close friends, infiltrating even the interactions between acquaintances.

In the aftermath of such a traumatic event, the pervasive divisions that emerged from ethnic tensions profoundly influenced how individuals perceived and interacted with one another. Even at the initial stage of acquaintance, biases rooted in ethnic background often dictated how individuals were perceived and approached. These biases were deeply ingrained, shaped by the traumatic experiences of the genocide and the societal divisions that followed.

For instance, a friend once confided in me about attending an event where she felt deeply moved and on the verge of tears. However, she hesitated to express her emotions openly, particularly in the presence of individuals from Hutu backgrounds. This hesitation stemmed from the lingering trauma of the genocide, which had instilled a sense of fear and mistrust, making even the simple act of expressing emotions a daunting task.

The scars of the past continued to cast a shadow over interpersonal interactions, influencing behavior and shaping perceptions. Recognizing the urgent need to address these deep-seated divisions, the Rwandan government implemented various initiatives to foster a sense of national identity that transcended ethnic differences. One such initiative, NDI UMUNYARWANDA, sought to promote unity and reconciliation by emphasizing our shared Rwandan identity above all else.

Through educational programs, community dialogues, and cultural events, these initiatives encouraged individuals to see themselves first and foremost as Rwandans, bound together by a common history and shared aspirations for the future. Indeed, before identifying as members of a particular ethnic group, we are first and foremost human beings bound together by our shared humanity. Regardless of our ethnic backgrounds, our relationships with acquaintances hold inherent value and significance.

By recognizing and embracing our shared humanity, we can break down the barriers that once divided us, fostering genuine connections and building a more inclusive and cohesive society. In essence, the journey toward reconciliation and healing requires us to transcend the divisions of the past and embrace a vision of unity that celebrates our shared identity as Rwandans.

Through empathy, understanding, and a commitment to building bridges across ethnic lines (remember that we cannot really even talk about ethnic groups in the case of Rwanda), we can forge a future where the wounds of the past no longer dictate the course of our relationships.

As we navigate this path toward reconciliation, remember that our shared humanity is the foundation for building a brighter, more inclusive future for all Rwandans.

As you can see, these initial relationships are significant, and it's essential to approach them with intentionality and awareness. By following the principles of respectful engagement and mutual understanding, we can foster meaningful connections and unlock the full potential of our interactions with acquaintances.

Here are a few principles to help you navigate acquaintances effectively and derive maximum value from these initial connections.

Respect and Courtesy: The foundation of any relationship, including those with acquaintances, is built upon respect and courtesy. Even though acquaintances may not be as intimately involved in our lives as close friends or family, treating them with politeness, attentiveness, and consideration is essential. Simple gestures like greeting them warmly, actively listening to what they say, and showing appreciation for their presence can go a long way in fostering positive interactions. By extending respect and courtesy to acquaintances, we create an environment of mutual respect and goodwill, laying the groundwork for potential future connections.

Respect Differences: Acquaintances, like individuals in any social setting, come from diverse backgrounds and hold varying beliefs and experiences. It's crucial to approach these differences with an open mind and a willingness to learn. Avoid making assumptions or judgments based on superficial characteristics and instead, seek to understand and appreciate the unique perspectives of others. Embracing diversity enriches our social interactions and broadens our understanding of the world, ultimately fostering greater empathy and connection with those around us.

Mind Your First Impressions: The significance of first impressions cannot be overstated, especially in the context of acquaintanceships that have the potential to evolve into more meaningful relationships. As the initial point of contact, strive to create positive impressions by projecting warmth, friendliness, and reliability. Whether it's a brief encounter or a more extended interaction, demonstrating genuine interest and respect for the other person sets the stage for future rapport and engagement.

Remember, the way we present ourselves in the beginning can significantly influence the trajectory of our relationships with acquaintances.

Maintain Boundaries: While being open and approachable in our interactions with acquaintances is essential, maintaining appropriate boundaries is equally important. Acquaintances may have different emotional investment or availability levels than close friends or family members. Avoid oversharing personal information or expecting them to fulfill the same support roles reserved for intimate relationships. By respecting boundaries and understanding the nature of acquaintanceships, we can navigate these relationships with sensitivity and respect for each other's boundaries.

Treat Others (Acquaintances) as You Would Want to Be Treated: While often recognized as a guiding principle for all relationships, the *"Golden Rule"* holds particular relevance in acquaintanceships as the foundational basis for establishing rapport and mutual respect. At its core, the "Golden Rule" embodies the principle of treating others as we wish to be treated, emphasizing empathy, kindness, and consideration in our interactions with acquaintances.

Unlike relationships governed by explicit agreements or formal contracts, where obligations are delineated, acquaintanceships operate more informally and intuitively, rooted in mutual understanding and goodwill. For example, in professional settings, adherence to the terms of a contract or agreement is essential for defining expectations and responsibilities. However, beyond these formal obligations lies the broader principle of the "Golden Rule," which encourages individuals to approach their interactions with acquaintances with empathy and respect, irrespective of contractual obligations.

Similarly, while a strong sense of commitment and love shapes personal relationships like marriage, following the "Golden Rule" is a guiding principle for fostering mutual understanding and consideration.

The "Golden Rule" underscores the importance of empathy and compassion in all human interactions, particularly in the initial stages of acquaintanceships, where impressions are formed and relationships are cultivated. By embodying these values from the outset, individuals can establish trust and mutual respect, laying the groundwork for meaningful and harmonious relationships with acquaintances and beyond.

Networking: Acquaintances offer valuable networking opportunities that benefit personal and professional growth. Recognizing and leveraging these connections can open new possibilities, insights, and resources. Whether seeking career advice, exploring new interests, or expanding your social circle, acquaintances can serve as valuable sources of support and information. By nurturing these connections and staying open to potential collaborations or exchanges, we maximize the potential for growth and enrichment in our personal and professional lives.

"In an actual sense, it's not that you should treat others as you would want to be treated; on the contrary, at the end of the day, you will surely be treated as you treat others."

CHAPTER 8
THE HEALING JOURNEY: STRATEGIES AND PRACTICES

In our ongoing exploration of Healing and Growth, it is paramount that we pause to reflect deeply on our progress, particularly in the aftermath of such profound trauma as genocide.

Throughout our discussions, we have delved into the intricacies of mastering relationships, rebuilding lives, and moving forward. However, paying attention to the pivotal aspect of Healing from a holistic perspective would be significant. This chapter serves as a poignant reminder to consider where we stand on this arduous journey toward wholeness and well-being.

The road to Healing is often fraught with uncertainty and doubt, especially for those who have endured the horrors of the 94 genocide against the Tutsi.

You may find yourself grappling with the concept of "normalcy," questioning why the process seems protracted or elusive. It is crucial to acknowledge that surviving such a traumatic event is an extraordinary challenge that demands immense strength, resilience, and patience.

You might wonder why it takes so long to return to a sense of normalcy, or perhaps you're unsure what "normal" even means. Surviving a traumatic event like the genocide against the Tutsi is an immense challenge, one that leaves lasting scars on the soul, one that demands immense resilience and patience. However, it's essential to recognize that Healing is not a destination but rather a journey—a journey that, with time and effort, can lead to newfound strength. Yet, this process isn't as simple as flipping a switch; it requires careful planning and strategic efforts, much like building a house brick by brick rather than watching a bush grow wild.

Dr. Myles Munroe's analogy of a garden versus a bush offers profound insights into the nature of Healing. Just as tending to a garden requires meticulous planning and effort, so does the healing process. It is not a passive endeavor but an intentional journey toward restoration and renewal.

Like a skilled gardener, we must carefully nurture the seeds of Healing within ourselves, cultivating an environment conducive to Growth and transformation.

The scars left by the 94 genocide against the Tutsi run deep, leaving indelible marks on individuals' mental, physical, and emotional well-being. Recovering from such trauma demands a comprehensive approach, one that acknowledges the complexity of survivors' experiences and addresses their unique needs with compassion and understanding.

It is a journey fraught with challenges and setbacks but promises profound Healing and resilience.

Yet, as we embark on this journey, we must confront a sobering reality: the transgenerational transmission of trauma. Many individuals born after the genocide find themselves grappling with the same symptoms and struggles as those who lived through it firsthand.

Consider, for instance, the poignant story of a 12-year-old boy in the diaspora, haunted by the specter of violence despite his limited exposure to its aftermath. His experience underscores the insidious nature of trauma inheritance and the profound impact it can have across generations.

Such occurrences beg the question: How does this trauma persist across generations?

Dr. Clarisse Musanabaganwa's groundbreaking research delves into the molecular mechanisms underlying this phenomenon, offering invaluable insights into the biological underpinnings of PTSD and trauma.

She embarked on an investigation into the intergenerational transmission of trauma following the 94 Genocide against the Tutsi. Inspired by the findings of Professor Yehuda Rachel's studies on the Holocaust, she sought to understand how the echoes of past horrors reverberated through the genetic tapestry of survivors and their descendants.

Using cutting-edge epigenomic technology, She delved into the molecular mechanisms underlying the inheritance of trauma. Epigenomic studies evaluate how environmental factors, such as exposure to traumatic events and chemicals, impact gene transcription without altering the genetic codes themselves.

Dr. Clarisse and her colleagues recruited women who had survived the genocide while pregnant in 1994, along with their offspring, as well as a control group of women who were not present in the country during the genocide and their children. She meticulously screened them for symptoms of Post-Traumatic Stress Disorder (PTSD) and its related conditions.

Simultaneously, Dr. Clarisse collected blood samples and extracted DNA, enabling advanced molecular analysis focused on DNA methylation—an epigenetic marker.

The data revealed a striking correlation: women who had experienced the genocide and their children exhibited higher levels of PTSD symptoms and epigenetic changes compared to the control group. These epigenetic alterations were linked to the transmission of trauma across generations.

Dr. Clarisse's findings shed light on the profound impact of trauma at the molecular level, suggesting that parents may transmit markers of trauma epigenetically to their children.

These discoveries compelled her to expand her study, recruiting a total of 450 participants—both genocide survivors and matched controls—to explore further the enduring legacy of trauma and its implications for future generations.

This investigation of how environmental factors shape our genetic expression sheds light on the intergenerational transmission of trauma. These findings not only deepen our understanding of trauma's far-reaching effects but also pave the way for targeted interventions to break the cycle of suffering and promote healing.

To put it simply, trauma can leave a kind of "mark" on our genes. These aren't changes to the DNA itself but rather changes to how our genes are turned on or off. Think of it like sticky notes that tell certain genes to be more active or less active. These sticky notes can be added because of stress and trauma, and they can even be passed down to the next generation.

However, here's the good news: just as these marks can be added, they can also be removed or altered when the environment changes. Studies have shown that positive, supportive, and nurturing environments can help erase these negative marks. For instance, when individuals are exposed to caring and stress-free environments, the negative effects of trauma on gene expression can be diminished or even reversed.

Research supports this hopeful outlook. One notable study from the University of California, San Francisco, found that nurturing maternal behavior could reverse some of the negative effects of early-life stress on gene expression. In this study, rats that experienced early-life stress but were later raised by nurturing mothers showed changes in the epigenetic marks on a key stress-regulating gene, leading to normalized stress responses.

Similarly, a study published in the journal "Biological Psychiatry" highlighted how supportive social environments can mitigate the epigenetic effects of early trauma. This study examined children who had been adopted from institutions where they experienced neglect and compared them to children raised in more supportive environments. The researchers found that the adopted children who received higher levels of parental care and support showed fewer negative epigenetic changes associated with stress and trauma, suggesting that a nurturing environment can indeed promote resilience and healing.

Moreover, research on mindfulness and meditation has shown that these practices can positively affect gene expression. A study published in "Psychoneuroendocrinology" found that individuals who engaged in mindfulness meditation exhibited changes in the expression of genes involved in inflammation and stress response. This suggests that mindfulness practices can help counteract the negative epigenetic effects of stress and trauma, promoting overall mental and physical health.

Additionally, studies on physical activity have demonstrated its beneficial effects on gene expression. Regular exercise has been shown to influence the expression of genes related to brain function and mood regulation. For example, a study published in "Translational Psychiatry" found that physical activity could reverse some of the negative epigenetic changes associated with stress, highlighting the importance of a healthy lifestyle in promoting resilience.

When individuals are exposed to supportive, nurturing, and stress-free environments, the negative epigenetic marks left by trauma can be diminished or even erased. These findings are backed by substantial research in the field of epigenetics, demonstrating the power of positive environmental changes in promoting healing and resilience.

The research from the University of California, San Francisco, on nurturing maternal behavior, underscores the potential for parental care to reverse stress-induced epigenetic changes. Likewise, the study published in "Biological Psychiatry" on children adopted from neglectful environments highlights how supportive social environments can mitigate the effects of early trauma.

Moreover, the findings from "Psychoneuroendocrinology" on mindfulness meditation and the "Translational Psychiatry" study on physical activity further validate the role of positive lifestyle practices in counteracting the negative epigenetic impacts of stress and trauma.

These studies collectively illustrate that while trauma can leave lasting biochemical marks on our DNA, these marks are not immutable. The environments and experiences we encounter throughout our lives continue to shape our gene expression, offering opportunities for healing and recovery.

By fostering supportive, nurturing, and stress-free environments, we can create the conditions necessary for reversing the epigenetic imprints of trauma and promoting overall well-being.

In conclusion, the evidence supports the notion that the epigenetic transmission of trauma can be undone through positive environmental changes. This empowers us to take proactive steps towards creating environments that promote healing and resilience. Through targeted interventions, mental health support, and broader social policies, we can work towards breaking the cycle of suffering and fostering a healthier, more resilient future for all generations.

As we navigate the complexities of Healing and rebuilding in the aftermath of the 94 genocide, it's imperative to consider the impact on all generations, including the unborn. Many individuals may struggle to comprehend the origins and implications of their trauma, highlighting the need for comprehensive support and guidance. The challenges faced by survivors and their descendants are complex and multifaceted, requiring a nuanced understanding of trauma's enduring legacy.

In the pages ahead, we'll explore the various phases of Healing that many survivors encounter on their journey to thriving. We can chart a path toward resilience and empowerment by gaining insight into our experiences and understanding where we stand.

The First phase of survival is to get to the place of Safety and Security:

Establishing safety is paramount for survivors of genocide. This is what began 30 years ago, thanks to Inkotanyi. Many may have experienced displacement, loss of homes, and ongoing threats to their safety. Finding a secure living environment and meeting basic needs are essential first steps in the healing process.

This phase may have been going on for the last 30 years because each person will see safety and security differently. Yes, since July 94, many feel safe. There are probably no more life-threatening situations, but safety is not just about not being hunted down; it is a sense of ease in life. When your mind does not feel entirely safe, there are many things that you cannot express. You are in survival mode if you are still looking for safety.

This is very important to understand because, for an extended period, you felt numb to pain or grief and did not allow yourself to even be sad, always on the go.

At some point, you are wondering why you are softening, have started crying, and feel a void. That is because you are now in a safe space. Only when your subconscious mind decides that you are safe can it start releasing the contained emotions and all that has hurt you.

One of my friends who was in the republican guard, the branch of the Rwanda Defence Force that has the responsibility to protect the president and other VIPs, was telling me how, in April 1995, during the first commemoration of the 94 Genocide held at Rebero, he was on duty. The person giving testimonies was from his neighborhood, talking about what happened to his family. Still, because at that time, my friend was on duty, protecting the president, he did not even think about what was being shared concerning his own family. He was not yet in the safe space; his concern was protecting the event.

Since then, he has started his own flourishing company and different businesses and has been hustling for the last 30 years. Only on April 7, 2024, when H.E, the president, was sharing about his own family who was killed during the 94 genocide against the Tutsi, did my friend actually start crying.

Of course, coming from the Republican Guard, it took him 30 years to be in a safe space.

When he saw his former boss, the president, allowing himself to be vulnerable enough to share a personal story, he felt allowed to feel and express his emotions, too. My point is that some may be feeling things they have never felt and are wondering what is happening; you are now in a safe space, and many restrained and repressed emotions are coming out; it is now time to give them room and voice because you can not contain them forever.

It's only once you have found safety and security that you can move on to the next phase of Healing, that is:

Dealing with Grief and Loss:
The scale of loss in the 94 genocide against the Tutsi is immense, encompassing the loss of family, friends, community, and cultural identity.

You need a safe space and support to grieve these profound losses. Do whatever is enough for you to grieve according to you. There is no one way to do this: do what you feel is right. Some people have different rituals and cultural practices but make your own.

Community support plays a crucial role in the grieving process, providing opportunities for remembrance and honoring those we lost. But as many have said, some people have dealt with their share of collective memorializing but have not yet dealt with their grief. This is very dangerous, so pace yourself on your personal journey. This phase is particularly painful for those who have no idea where their loved ones were killed. Many people have not found the bodies of their family members, and it is very hard to begin to grieve the loss when you always think they may be alive somewhere, still hoping, being strong and courageous.

When you fully experience and process your grief, you are more likely to reach a place of acceptance and resolution. This process involves acknowledging the loss's pain, expressing associated emotions, and gradually integrating the experience into your life story.

Through this journey of grieving, you can come to terms with the reality of the loss, honor the memory of what or who was lost, **and ultimately find a sense of closure that allows you to move forward and thrive in life.**

Finding closure in the context of the 94 genocide against the Tutsi, perpetrated by neighbors and trusted individuals, adds a layer of complexity to the grieving process. The betrayal and loss of trust experienced in this situation will intensify anger, resentment, and disbelief, making it even more challenging to come to terms with the reality of the loss.

It's normal to struggle with conflicting emotions, torn between the memories of the past and the need to move forward with your life.

Closure in this context will involve:

- Confronting the painful truths of betrayal and loss.
- Acknowledging the complexity of human nature.
- Finding a way to reconcile your past with the present.

It will definitely require grappling with difficult questions about forgiveness, justice, and reconciliation and finding a way to honor the memory of those who have been lost while still holding individuals accountable for their actions.

One of the critical challenges in finding closure in the context of the 94 genocide against the Tutsi is the need to navigate the complex dynamics of community relationships and social identity that sometimes include mixed family contexts. You may even struggle with guilt or shame associated with the perpetrators' actions and fears of retaliation or ostracism from their families or communities. This can further complicate the grieving process and hinder the ability to find closure.

Despite these challenges, closure is still possible. It may involve seeking support from trusted friends, family members, or mental health professionals (this one is significant) who can provide a safe space to explore and process difficult emotions. It may also involve engaging in healing practices such as storytelling, memorialization, or community rituals that honor the memory of the victims and provide a sense of collective Healing and solidarity.

Ultimately, finding closure requires courage, resilience, and a willingness to confront the painful truths of the past. By embracing the healing journey with compassion and determination, you will find a sense of peace and resolution that honors the memory of those who have been lost while paving the way for a brighter future.

Closure is essential because it is the only pathway to emotional Healing. It provides a sense of resolution and completeness to the grieving process, allowing you to even think about moving forward with life. It helps to alleviate the emotional burden associated with unresolved feelings of grief, anger, or guilt.

Closure promotes Psychological Well-being by reducing distress and promoting inner peace. It allows one not to be imprisoned by the past and to focus on the present moment and future possibilities.

Of course, as we have already discussed, closure will positively impact relationships by helping you navigate your emotions and communicate more effectively with others. It will lead to healthier interactions and foster deeper connections with loved ones.

Only closure will allow your total personal Growth. Finding closure often involves reflecting on the lessons learned from the experience of loss or trauma. This can contribute to personal Growth and resilience as you better understand yourself and your capacity to overcome adversity.

Closure is essential for moving forward with life after experiencing such profound loss.

It allows you to release feelings of guilt, anger, or regret that may hinder your ability to live fully in the present and plan for the future.

The 94 Genocide against the Tusti has disrupted the fabric of families and our communities, leaving many grappling with feelings of uncertainty and instability. Closure can restore stability by providing a sense of resolution and closure, allowing you to regain control over your life.

Unresolved grief and trauma can have long-term consequences for mental health. By achieving closure, you can mitigate the risk of developing mental health issues such as depression, anxiety, or post-traumatic stress disorder (PTSD). Remember that according to the Rwanda Biomedical Centre (RBC), one in five Rwandans has one or more signs of mental health issues.

In essence, closure is crucial to navigating the complex emotions and challenges associated with loss and to ultimately find peace and Healing in the aftermath of such a tragedy.

Moving forward from surviving the 94 genocide against the Tutsi to thriving involves merging processing individual losses to addressing the broader impact of trauma on mental health and well-being.

After addressing grief and loss, it's essential to acknowledge the collective trauma experienced by survivors of the 94 genocide against the Tutsi. This involves recognizing the widespread psychological and emotional effects of living through such extreme violence and loss.

We need to integrate into our lives some trauma-informed care and an understanding of Trauma Responses.

Trauma-informed care involves understanding how individuals respond to traumatic events and how these responses may manifest in their behavior, emotions, and relationships.

It's normal for survivors of the genocide to exhibit a range of trauma responses, including hypervigilance, avoidance, and emotional numbing; as a society, we need to give room for all of these emotions.

We must emphasize the importance of creating safe and supportive environments for survivors to heal. This will involve providing and encouraging access to mental health resources, support groups, and culturally sensitive therapy modalities. As a society, we definitely need to remove all the stigmas around mental health and all trauma reactions.

We need to empower survivors more and more by validating each one's experience without comparing anyone's journey, promoting autonomy, and fostering a sense of agency in each one's healing journey. This can sometimes involve collaborative goal-setting, decision-making, and advocacy for survivors' needs and rights.

As a society, we need to integrate trauma-focused therapies, mindfulness practices, and expressive arts therapies into our culture. We must acknowledge the importance of cultural competence and sensitivity in supporting survivors from diverse backgrounds. This includes understanding the cultural context of the 94 genocide against the Tutsi, finding different ways to help in the trauma healing journey that integrates our cultural beliefs and practices, and adapting interventions to be culturally responsive.

Having more professionals who understand the complexities of trauma specific to the 94 genocide against the Tutsi is vital. We need more specialized therapists, counselors, or support groups that focus on the 94 genocide against the Tutsi survivors and can offer culturally sensitive approaches to Healing. This Trauma-informed care has to emphasize safety, trustworthiness, choice, collaboration, and empowerment in the therapeutic process.

Integrating personal grief and loss processing with trauma-informed care provides survivors of the 94 genocide against the Tutsi with a holistic approach to addressing the profound psychological and emotional impacts of their experiences. By recognizing the importance of allowing individuals to grieve their losses in their own way and time, we honor the uniqueness of each survivor's journey.

This personal grieving process is essential for acknowledging and processing the immense scale of loss—of our family, friends, community, and cultural identity—that we have endured.

Simultaneously, trauma-informed care offers a framework for understanding and responding to the broader psychological and emotional effects of trauma.

It emphasizes safety, trustworthiness, choice, collaboration, and empowerment, recognizing the widespread impact of trauma and its potential to shape individuals' beliefs, behaviors, and interactions. By integrating trauma-informed principles into care practices, many will receive the comprehensive support and resources they need to navigate the complex terrain of trauma recovery.

Together, these approaches create a supportive environment that fosters Healing and resilience.

Survivors are empowered to explore their trauma, process their emotions, and develop coping strategies in a safe and compassionate space. By combining personal grief work with trauma-informed care, we honor the past, validate our experiences, and pave the way for a brighter future filled with hope, connection, and possibility. This is paramount to moving from survival to thriving, "Kudadira, or Kwiyubaka," as we say.

Transitioning from trauma-informed care to community support, survivors of the 94 genocide against the Tutsi can find solace and strength in connecting with others who share similar experiences.

Rebuilding your life after such profound trauma requires more than individual resilience—it requires the support and understanding of a community that can offer empathy, validation, and solidarity. On this journey to recover and rebuild your life, connecting with others who understand your experiences is essential.

Building or reconnecting with a supportive community can give you the understanding and empathy you need to navigate the complexities of Healing and recovery. Organizations like IBUKA, AVEGA Agahozo, AERG, and GAERG offer valuable resources, support, and camaraderie.

Participating in community events, support groups, and cultural practices can foster a sense of belonging and connection, helping you feel less isolated in your experiences.

As you embark on your journey of Healing and recovery, remember that you are not alone. Reach out to others who understand your journey and can offer you the support and solidarity you need to rebuild your life. Together, we can create a community of Healing and hope that uplifts and empowers each other on the path to wholeness.

That said, it's essential to recognize that everyone's journey is unique, and what works for one person may not necessarily work for another. Respecting each person's autonomy and choices regarding their healing process is crucial, and support should be offered in a way that is sensitive to their needs and preferences.

You decide to share or withhold traumatic experiences from others, including your family members; do all at your own pace and comfort. This is deeply personal and can be influenced by various psychological, social, and relational factors. You need to have agency over your own narratives and choose what feels safest and most supportive for your healing journey. Do not feel pressured in any way.

However, as a society, we must also create a safe space to address the barriers preventing survivors from sharing their experiences. Creating a supportive and understanding environment where everyone feels safe and comfortable opening up is essential. Here are some ways to avoid or mitigate these barriers:

Increase awareness and understanding among family members about the different and unique psychological effects of trauma and the challenges some survivors may face in sharing their experiences. Education can help reduce stigma, foster empathy, and encourage supportive responses.

Not everyone processes trauma like everyone else. We have to remember that the 94 genocide against the Tutsi has many different aspects that can make it difficult for some to conform to what many other survivors do.

In some situations, survivors may worry about how others, including their own family members, will react to their experiences and fear being judged or criticized. They may anticipate negative reactions or blame, leading them to keep their experiences to themselves. We need to foster an environment of open communication within the family where feelings, experiences, and concerns can be shared openly and without judgment. Encourage family members and the community to listen to and validate each other's experiences actively. Not everyone has gone through this the same way, and no traumatic experience is less than the other. As they say, grief is singular; grief and trauma are recognized as highly individualized experiences.

Each person's experience of grief and trauma is unique and influenced by various factors such as personality, coping mechanisms, past experiences, and different family or even cultural backgrounds.

It is very common that some just want to keep quiet to shield their family members from the pain and trauma of their experiences, especially when this involves things like rape. They may believe that sharing their stories will burden their loved ones with emotional distress or guilt, and they may choose to keep their experiences private to protect their family members from further harm; we always need to keep this in mind when dealing with ourselves and respect each one's boundaries and autonomy in deciding when and how they want to share their experiences. Avoid pressuring anyone to disclose their trauma before they feel ready, and let them know that it's okay to take their time.

IT IS OKAY TO TAKE YOUR TIME AND DO THINGS AT YOUR OWN PACE

Talking about traumatic experiences like the genocide can be re-traumatizing for some, mainly if they have not yet processed or come to terms with their trauma. Some family or friends may avoid sharing their experiences with us to prevent triggering painful memories or emotions associated with the trauma. Let's offer them access to different supportive resources such as therapy, support groups, and counseling services. These resources can provide a safe space for many to process their experiences and receive validation and support from others than ourselves, either because they have gone through similar situations or because they are professionals who can help better than we can.

Did you know that some survivors may experience feelings of shame or guilt about their experiences, mainly if they believe they could have done something differently to prevent the trauma? These feelings can lead them to hide their experiences from their loved ones, as they may fear being perceived as weak or flawed.

We must be the first to create safe spaces within the family where everyone feels comfortable sharing their experiences without fear of judgment or re-traumatization. Foster an atmosphere of trust, respect, and acceptance where everyone's voices are heard and valued.

Lead by example and model healthy communication and coping strategies within the family. Demonstrate empathy, active listening, and validation in your interactions with others, and encourage family members to do the same.

Also, some may come from families with dysfunctional or abusive dynamics, where sharing personal experiences is discouraged or punished. They may have learned from past experiences that it is unsafe to be vulnerable or open with their family members, leading them to keep their experiences to themselves. If underlying issues or dysfunctional dynamics within the family may impede communication and support, consider seeking professional help or family therapy to address these issues in a constructive and supportive manner.

By implementing these strategies, and many others I may not have touched on, we can create a supportive and understanding environment where all survivors feel empowered to share their experiences and receive the support they need for Healing and recovery. We need to thrive as a society and not leave anyone behind.

Many survivors have experienced physical injuries or chronic stress-related conditions.

Addressing physical health issues and appearance is essential for overall well-being.

One of my friends only recently decided to undergo surgery for aesthetic issues borne for decades. Accessing medical care, practicing self-care, and engaging in physical activities will contribute to and promote Healing and resilience.

In addition to personal Healing, **engaging with legal justice and advocacy** is a significant aspect of the journey towards recovery and rebuilding after surviving the 94 genocide against the Tutsi.

While the scale of atrocities committed during the genocide may seem impossible, seeking justice for the crimes perpetrated against individuals and communities is an essential step toward accountability and closure.

Pursuing legal justice is a means of reclaiming agency and dignity in the face of profound loss and injustice. It is a way to honor the memory of those we lost and prevent similar atrocities from happening in the future. However, it's important to acknowledge that engaging with legal processes can also be fraught with challenges and potential re-traumatization.

Navigating the legal system, especially internationally, requires expertise and support. Legal professionals who specialize in genocide-related cases can provide invaluable assistance in understanding complex legal issues, advocating for survivors' rights, and seeking redress for the crimes committed. Here is where different survivor support organizations and advocacy groups can offer guidance, resources, and solidarity throughout the legal journey.

It's crucial to approach legal justice and advocacy with realistic expectations and to prioritize your well-being throughout the process.

While achieving legal accountability for genocide may be a long and arduous journey, every step taken toward truth and justice contributes to the collective Healing of our communities and nation.

Ultimately, legal justice and advocacy are integral to the broader healing journey. We reclaim our voices, stories, and humanity in the face of unimaginable suffering by seeking accountability for past atrocities and advocating for a more just and compassionate world.

As we continue this healing journey, we must address another significant aspect:

Psychological Integration.

Integrating the experience of genocide into your life story is a complex and deeply personal process. It involves finding ways to acknowledge the trauma and its profound impact without allowing it to define your entire identity.

This process requires courage, self-reflection, and a willingness to confront painful memories and emotions.

One key element of psychological integration is self-awareness. By gaining a deeper understanding of how the genocide has shaped your thoughts, beliefs, and behaviors, you can begin to untangle its influence from your sense of self. This may involve exploring how trauma has affected your relationships, worldview, and understanding of safety in the world.

Seeking guidance from mental health professionals who specialize in trauma recovery can be immensely helpful during this process. Therapists and counselors can provide a safe and supportive space for you to explore your experiences, express your emotions, and develop coping strategies for managing the lingering effects of trauma.

It's important to remember that psychological integration is not about forgetting or denying the past. Instead, it's about finding a way to incorporate your experiences into the broader narrative of your life in a way that allows you to move forward with strength and resilience. This may involve reframing your perspective, finding meaning amid suffering, and reclaiming agency over your story.

By embracing the process of psychological integration, you can begin to heal the wounds of the past and create a new narrative of hope, Growth, and possibility for the future.

Moving forward on your healing journey, we come to another crucial phase: Finding Meaning and Purpose.

For many survivors, finding Healing means finding meaning in their suffering. Engaging in activities that prevent future atrocities or educate others about genocide can provide a profound sense of purpose and contribution to the greater good.

Whether it's through writing, speaking, activism, or other forms of advocacy, survivors have the opportunity to use their experiences to make a positive impact on the world.

Finding meaning and purpose beyond your own life is essential for moving from merely surviving to thriving. It's about recognizing that your life has significance beyond your survival and that you have the power to make a meaningful contribution to the world around you. This sense of purpose can serve as a guiding light, helping you navigate the challenges of your healing journey with courage and determination.

Discovering your purpose may involve exploring your values, passions, and strengths. What issues or causes resonate deeply with you? What talents or skills do you possess that can be used to effect positive change? By aligning your actions with your values and goals, you can create a life rich in meaning and fulfillment.

It's important to remember that finding meaning and purpose is not a one-time event but an ongoing process.

As you continue on your healing journey, you may discover new passions, interests, and growth opportunities. Embrace these opportunities with an open heart and mind, knowing each step brings you closer to a life of purpose and significance.

Finding meaning and purpose in your suffering can transform your experiences into a source of strength and inspiration. You are not defined by what happened to you but by how you choose to respond to it. Embrace your power to create positive change in the world, find purpose in your pain, and make an impact that transcends the boundaries of your own life.

Let your journey from surviving to thriving be a beacon of hope and inspiration for others.

As we delve deeper into Healing and purpose, **I cannot overlook the role of faith, particularly the connection with God.** Many have found solace and strength in their faith and dedication to God during profound suffering and loss.

I can only talk about Healing and purpose by acknowledging the profound impact of faith. We may need help understanding or finding logical explanations for many things, especially when grappling with questions of why and how. Yet, even amid uncertainty, I have witnessed and experienced God's transformative power.

While God may not always explain our pain and suffering, He often reveals Himself unexpectedly, offering comfort, guidance, and hope to those who seek Him.

As my brother, Myles Munroe Jr, said after the plane crash that killed both his parents, Dr. Myles Munroe, and his wife, Ruth Ann Munroe, even If God may not explain Himself, He will definitely express Himself, and He indeed did.

Reconnecting with God can be a profound source of comfort and support as you navigate the complexities of Healing from trauma and finding a sense of purpose because, as I believe God has created us, your purpose can only be found in your creator's mind. So reconnecting to God is the way to tap into this supernatural realm. Honestly, I do not know how anyone can make it without God.

Finding your way to connect or reconnect with God can provide peace and reassurance in the face of immense loss and trauma. Also, this offers a sense of community and connection, providing opportunities to share your experiences with others with similar beliefs and values.

In times of crisis, coming together with fellow believers can be incredibly healing, offering mutual support, encouragement, and solidarity on your journey toward Healing and wholeness.

Ultimately, faith provides a sense of continuity and meaning in the face of life's greatest challenges. Grounding yourself in your faith and trusting in God can help you find strength and resilience to overcome even the most daunting obstacles.

As you embark on your healing journey, may you find solace and strength in your faith, knowing that you are never alone and that no matter what, God guides you every step!

Before we conclude this conversation, I want to emphasize the importance of **ongoing support and self-care on this healing journey.**

As you continue to navigate the complexities of Healing from trauma, it's crucial to recognize that you can not walk this journey alone.

Surrounding yourself with a network of support from mental health professionals, community groups, friends, and family members is essential for long-term Healing and well-being. These individuals can provide invaluable guidance, encouragement, and understanding as you work through the challenges and triumphs of your healing journey.

I want to stress that seeking support is not a sign of weakness but a courageous step towards Healing.

Too often, in our culture, some people feel ashamed or hesitant to ask for help; we have sayings like" imfura ishinjagira ishira," saying that you must keep your head high even when you can barely walk; this is not right when it comes to dealing with traumatic situation like what we went through in 94 genocide against the Tutsi. We need to stop judgment or stigma around mental health. Reaching out for support is a testament to your strength and resilience, showing that you are willing to confront your pain and take proactive steps toward Healing.

Self-care practices also play a vital role in promoting wellness and resilience in the face of trauma. Taking time for yourself and engaging in activities that nourish your mind, body, and spirit is not selfish—it's necessary. Whether practicing mindfulness techniques, engaging in physical exercise, or simply taking a moment to breathe deeply and center yourself, prioritizing self-care allows you to recharge and replenish your energy reserves. Listen, you owe nobody your life; it is a gift and another chance you have; take it and own it.

Furthermore, I want to emphasize the importance of maintaining a continuous connection with God, the creator. In times of struggle and uncertainty, your faith can be a steadfast source of comfort, guidance, and strength. Cultivating a daily connection, whether through prayer, reading His word, meditation, or reflection, allows you to stay grounded in your faith and find solace in the presence of the Most High.

Remember, healing from trauma is not a linear process, and there will be ups and downs along the way. Be gentle with yourself, and remember it's okay to ask for help when needed.

By prioritizing ongoing support and self-care, you can empower yourself to navigate healing challenges with resilience, grace, and hope.

CHAPTER 9

CONCLUSION

Moving from surviving to thriving is a journey that traverses the depths of human resilience and the expanse of our collective spirit. Healing from the trauma inflicted by the 1994 genocide against the Tutsi is not merely a destination but a lifelong odyssey, demanding a holistic approach that tends to the physical, emotional, and spiritual dimensions of our well-being. Through a profound recognition of our unique challenges and an unwavering commitment to understanding them, we can chart a course toward Healing and resilience that honors the depth of our shared experience.

In the pages of this book, we have embarked on a voyage into the heart of Healing from genocide trauma, exploring its intricate tapestry and its profound impact on individuals and communities alike.

With a keen focus on rebuilding relationships—from reclaiming identity to nurturing familial bonds and professional connections—we have traversed the labyrinthine pathways of suffering and redemption, seeking solace amidst the rubble of our past.

Our exploration has led us through the labyrinth of psychological and emotional landscapes, where the echoes of trauma reverberate in the silent chambers of our souls. We have navigated the turbulent waters of grief and loss, finding refuge in the embrace of community and the resilience of the human spirit. Along the way, we have unearthed the seeds of meaning amidst the wreckage of suffering, forging a path toward redemption and renewal.

Yet, this journey is not one to be traversed alone. By offering a comprehensive framework for Healing and recovery, we aim to empower each other with the knowledge, understanding, and resources needed to embark on this transformative odyssey. Together, we acknowledge the strength and courage that reside within each of us as we confront the legacy of trauma and forge a new path forward.

As we stand on the threshold of the future, let us not forget the lessons of the past nor the resilience that has brought us to this moment. Let us prioritize our well-being and Healing, extending compassion and understanding to one another as we navigate the complexities of our shared journey. In our collective strength and solidarity, we find the courage to dream of a world where Healing is not a distant dream but a tangible reality.

Indeed, we have come a long way in the past three decades, a testament to the indomitable spirit of the Rwandan people.

Yet, our journey is far from over, and the challenges ahead demand our utmost dedication and resolve.

Together, we can rise to meet them, proving to the world and ourselves that even in the face of unimaginable adversity, the human spirit knows no bounds.

HEALING JOURNEY

We stand at a crossroads, poised on the threshold of possibility, our gaze fixed firmly on the horizon of our collective destiny. Indeed, the strides we have made as a nation over the past three decades serve as a testament to the Rwandan people's resilience, determination, and unwavering spirit. We have risen from the ashes of tragedy, our wings unfurling to embrace the promise of a brighter tomorrow.

Yet, as we bask in the glow of our accomplishments, let us not forget the arduous path that lies ahead. We still have a long way to go—a journey fraught with challenges, obstacles, and uncertainties. And yet, if history has taught us anything, nothing is impossible when we stand united in purpose and resolve.

In the face of adversity, we have dared to dream of a Rwanda where healing and reconciliation flourish, where the scars of the past serve as a testament to our resilience rather than a barrier to our future. This dream knows no boundaries, transcending the confines of geography and circumstance. And it is a dream that we must continue to nurture and cultivate, for it is in the pursuit of our dreams that we find the strength to overcome even the greatest of obstacles.

As we look to the future, let us do so with purpose and determination, knowing that the road ahead may be extended and challenging but that we are not alone in our journey.

Our African brothers and sisters stand beside us, their hearts beating in rhythm with ours, their dreams intertwined with our own. Together, we can show the world that if it can be done in Rwanda, a nation that has endured so much, then it is possible to make it anywhere—if only we give ourselves the tools.

And so, let us arm ourselves with courage, resilience, and unwavering determination as we march forward into the unknown. Let us draw strength from the lessons of our past, knowing that they have prepared us for the challenges that lie ahead. And let us never lose sight of the dream that has brought us this far—a dream of Rwanda and, indeed, a continent that shines brightly as a beacon of hope and possibility for all who dare to dream. Together, we will reach the summit of our aspirations, for in the unity of our purpose lies the power to transform our dreams into reality with the strength to overcome even the greatest obstacles.

Let us move forward with courage and conviction, knowing that we carry within us the seeds of hope and the promise of a brighter tomorrow.

We got this,
and
I will see you at the top!

BIOGRAPHY
HUBERT SUGIRA HATEGEKIMANA
RELATIONSHIP EXPERT

Hubert Sugira Hategekimana, the visionary and Host of Kigali Family Night, is a renowned relationship expert and cross-cultural leader whose life journey has taken him from Rwanda to Europe and Canada.

With expertise honed through extensive training in self-discovery and leadership development under the tutelage of the late Dr. Myles Munroe, a world-renowned government consultant and best-selling author, he is deeply committed to empowering individuals to build and nurture strong, healthy relationships.

Hubert's profound insights and wisdom help transform lives, guiding people through the complexities of personal and professional relationships to unlock their full potential.

Additionally, as the vice chairman of the International Third-World Leaders Association (ITWLA), he remains dedicated to positively impacting the development of his native continent, Africa.

Hubert attributes his success to the love, support, and wisdom of his best friend and wife, Jennifer. Fondly acknowledging her role, he proudly introduces her as the one and only mother to their three beautiful children, Kayla, Ketsia, and Klemes.

Through books, online presence, seminars, and coaching, he empowers individuals to reach their full potential and fosters a culture of love and understanding.

Website: Hategekimana.com
Email: info@Hategekimana.com
www.facebook.com/HubertSugira
YouTube: Hubert Sugira Hategekimana
Twitter: @HubertSugira
Instagram: @HubertSugira

#WinAtHomeAndAway

www.ingramcontent.com/pod-product-compliance
Lightning Source LLC
Chambersburg PA
CBHW050107170426
43198CB00014B/2490